Symbolism

A TREATISE ON THE SOUL OF THINGS; HOW THE NATURAL WORLD IS BUT A SYMBOL OF THE REAL WORLD; THE MODERN CHURCH, WITH ITS SPIRE AND CROSS, AND THE BIBLE ACCOUNT OF NOAH'S ARK SYMBOLS OF THE PHALLIC RELIGION.

The Pack of Playing Cards, or Book of Fifty-two; An Ancient Masonic Bible; Each Card a Symbol of Universal Law; U.S.A. a Masonic Nation, whose Duty and History are Read in these Ancient Sacred Symbols; Ten Digits constituting our Mathematical System; Why they are Made in the Manner they are; Why there are but Ten; They and the Ten Spot Cards Reveal the same Psychic Laws; The Lost Word Revealed; Many Masonic Symbols; Biblical Expressions given a New and Natural Explanation.

Milton Alberto Pottenger

ISBN 1-56459-464-5

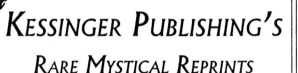

Yours Truly
Milton Alberto Pottenger

EDITOR'S PREFACE

SYMBOLISM

Little is known about MILTON ALBERTO POTTENGER, the original author of this book and as far as is known this was his only publication. The book was originally published in July of 1905 by the "SYMBOL PUBLISHING CO., SACRAMENTO, CA"; it was probably his own company as I have never located any other books from this publisher. Although he was most definitely a Mason, it is quite clear that this work is purely his own creation and does not seem to be affiliated with any Lodge or specific group. It has been suggested that he was a member of the Order of the Magi, but this is unlikely as much of his material is at odds with their teachings.

One important factor to re-publishing this work is that it is one of the few, if not the only book of this period, I have been able to locate which refers (on page 55) to the works of OLNEY H. RICHMOND and his 1893 'MYSTIC TEST BOOK" (republished in 1983 by Newcastle Publishing, Van Nuys, CA), the originator of what has become the ASTRO - CARDS System.

This book contains all of Pottenger's original text and charts unedited, except where I have had to fill in some of the characters that had faded. There are a few typographical and spelling errors but I think the reader will have no problem in following the text.

From Chart No. 2, page 188 onward, POTTENGER introduces various "Spreads" and some of their symbolism. It should be noted that he made some typographical errors with regard to these spreads. (The clue to converting the numbers given, comes from the Solar Value of each card: starting with A♥ = 1 up to K♥ = 13,

A♣ = 14 up to K♣ = 26, A♦ = 27 up to K♦ = 39, A♠ = 40 up to K♠ = 52.) As these Spreads on Chart No. 2 are so small, I have included a re-working of each of the 12 Zodiacal Spreads with the corrected numbers converted into their cards.

The illustrations he uses for the Court Cards are from a relatively old deck and in certain instances are facing in the opposite direction to the current designs of those cards; however, the pictorial integrity has been maintained, whether facing or looking away from their suit symbols. There has been merely a transposition of their designs, the engravers going from a positive picture to a negative reversal on the printing plate or vice versa.

The Quadration formula on pages 189 and 190 is not quite correct. The Deck should start face-down for the first part, and then turned over face-up before starting the second part of the process.

Another point to note is that Pottenger's Court Card - Astrological symbolism differs from that given by Richmond. Richmond gives the Zodiac order (Mystic Test Book, page 241) as

Capricorn K♠	Aries..... K♥	Cancer... K♣	Libra........ K♦
Aquarius.. Q♠	Taurus... Q♥	Leo........ Q♣	Scorpio.... Q♦
Pisces...... J♠	Gemini... J♥	Virgo..... J♣	Sagittarius J♦

whereas Pottenger has reversed the Kings and Jacks of each Triplicity. Personally I prefer Richmond's order as it gives the Kings to the Cardinal, the Queens to the Fixed and the Jacks to the Mutable signs, which makes good symbolic sense. However, I disagree with Richmond as to the Red Suits; I prefer that Diamonds should rule the second Triplicity (Aries, Taurus, Gemini) and that Hearts rule the fourth Triplicity (Libra, Scorpio, Sagittarius). There may be no right solution; each version merely reflecting an individual's world view and their cosmological interpretations of it through the language of Symbolism.

When reading this work realize that Pottenger is definitely a product of the late 19th century and this book should be read with that in mind as he had a totally different vision and understanding of the world compared to our current awarenesses. Since 1905, Science has given us so much more information about both the physical earth plane and our solar system. For example, the discovery of Pluto in the 1930's radically changes Pottenger's numerical/planet concepts; however, the metaphysical information when read in the appropriate manner is still valid.

Also be warned; when reading the Astrologically-related sections, Pottenger like Richmond, jumps between Heliocentric and Geocentric interpretations which can be a little confusing if one is not aware in advance.

Iain McLaren-Owens
Editor

DEDICATORY.

TO THOSE WHO HAVE OPEN AND RECEPTIVE MINDS, WILLING TO TAKE TRUTH BY THE HAND WHEREVER FOUND; TO THOSE "LITTLE CHILDREN" WHO, IT WAS DECLARED, ARE THE ONLY ONES PREPARED TO ENTER HEAVEN; TO THE MASONIC FRATERNITY; TO THE CITIZEN, AND TO THE STUDENT OF MYSTICISM THESE PAGES ARE RESPECTFULLY DEDICATED.

I HAVE WRITTEN, NOT FOR THOSE WHO KNOW, BUT FOR THOSE WHO DO NOT KNOW.

PREFACE.

N PRESENTING "Symbolism" to the world the author feels a sense of satisfaction in having accomplished a long cherished desire. The information contained herein, is not new to a few at least. Because of the prejudice of "the world," those who have been in possession of the light have hesitated to let it shine, knowing the time was not yet. It is expected that authorities will be searched to find the relation of Masonry to Playing Cards, but such authorities as the public will most frequently consult have themselves been misled. They have been obliged to assign some excuse for the existence of playing cards and not knowing the truth, have attributed their origin to the amusement of a foolish king, etc. One excuse is as good as another, however, when the real truth cannot be revealed, therefore the custodians of the light have permitted all sorts of misinformation to be circulated, knowing the true light would be revealed at the proper time. The truth teller is still in danger of social ostracism; not in danger as to personal liberty and life, however, as of yesterday. Humanity claims to have made wonderful progress, yet we read of a Christian nation asking God to assist it, by means of warfare, in its endeavors to annihilate another equally Christian nation. Brother is still arrayed against brother: each still believes in a personal God, subject to bribery and barter. Each still thinks of heaven as a locality, of hell an alleyway leading thereto.

Science has already reached the border land of materiality, her past domain, and is now stretching forth her hand into the realm of the psychic. Humanity itself, however, is fast becoming synthetical and scientific, and in order to retain their hold as teacher, and priest, and doctor, these professions must of a necessity find new fields of thought into which to lead their followers or lose their office.

Their cable tow of the past having about united with that of the immediate future they find themselves pushed off the mountain of error into the great realm of unknown truth—as yet unexplored—whose title may well be said to be "The Unknown Country."

The layman now lays aside faith and demands of the man of God that he prove his title by his works.

The doctor, claiming for his profession a scientific basis, is commanded to cease "practicing" and give positive results.

Symbolism is offered the public as a simple key. Its study and perusal will open to the "ripe" mind a store of unfathomable riches. It is hoped that by it many a soul will "see" the light, then "seek" and in "secrecy" find the truth of his own being.

NOTICE.

The two large charts embraced in this work may become torn and otherwise disfigured by much use and reference. Should the owner ever desire to replace them, or want duplicates for more convenient reference, the same can be had by addressing the publisher. The price is $2.00 for the two charts, shipping and handling included.

TABLE OF CONTENTS

————

A NARRATIVE

CHAPTER I.

The writer was raised in and about Chicago. In the month of March, 1884, President Arthur appointed me to take charge of the Indian school at Fort Hall, Ida., Mrs. Pottenger being named as matron. The position, it was stated, was non-political; my tenure of office would probably be of long duration since much difficulty had been experienced in getting a teacher to stay for any considerable period in that lonely locality. The only other white people at the fort were the sewing teacher and cook.

I took a deep interest in the work of teaching the Indian children; indeed, I enjoyed the duties more than any work I ever had before or since. We had been in our new position only six months, however, when we were discharged by President Cleveland.

White people were not allowed to live on the Fort Hall reservation. Our nearest neighbor was a man named George Howell, who lived across the Blackfoot river and several miles from the fort. In some manner, having learned of our discharge, he invited us to make his log cabin our home until we could locate ourselves. In a few weeks the door of another log cabin opened. "Dud" Gramer, a bachelor cowboy living up the Blackfoot river several miles, allowed that "if we would keep house and 'tend the ranch while he rode the range he would do the fair thing by us," so we took up our abode with him on what was known at that time as the "Shoemaker Ranch," it being owned by Judge Shoemaker of Blackfoot. While living here I received my first lessons in cowboy life as well as the art of trapping beaver. We had been on the ranch but a short time, however, when "Dud" informed me that he had "thrown up his contract and was going to quit the ranch." This, again, threw me upon the world with my wife and two little boys.

Two days later I was in Blackfoot City talking with the post-master, Joe Warren. In the course of our conversation I made known my condition. Mr. Warren said he had a good log house on a ranch down the river and placed it at my disposal. In a few days we moved from up the river fifteen miles above Blackfoot to down the river about five miles below that town. There was only one log cabin now between our house and the confluence of the Snake and Blackfoot rivers. At the point at which we lived the rivers were two miles apart. Along the Snake river there was a heavy growth of syca-more and cottonwood timber.

The cabin in which we lived, if still standing, will be found to contain six rooms, one built against the other. Doorways were cut from one room to the next. In early days Mr. Warren had built a toll bridge across the Blackfoot river at this point. He had erected a large log barn, and in his six-room house kept a supply of goods such as trappers, miners, cowboys, soldiers and Indians had need for. He also bought furs, gold dust, grain, vegetables and other products of the land.

In the very early days of Idaho Joe Warren's place was known for hundreds of miles. He was the justice of the peace, and as such was authorized to perform marriage ceremonies.

Being an illiterate man he had little regard for the English language and his marriage ceremony was unique if not the only one of its kind. In one of his six rooms Joe kept an excuse of a bar for the dissemination of "wet goods," and it was his wont to seal a trade or bargain of any kind by treating or being treated.

Marriages, of course, were few and far between on account of the great scarcity of the female sex; when a marriage did occur cowboys, Indians, trappers and miners for many miles around would congregate to witness the ceremony.

The company having gathered in the large Common room, so called on account of the large fireplace, Joe would stand the bride and groom in the center of the room. Taking the hand of the bride he would place it in that of the groom and addressing himself to her would say:

"Do you take this man to be your husband?" After receiving the customary timid "Yes, sir," he would then address the groom:

"Will you take this woman to be your wife?" Upon an affirmative reply being made he would say, "Well, then, I pronounce you man and wife, and if any fellow says you ain't he's a damn liar. Let's take a drink."

We spent the winter of 1884-5 in this log house. The first work I did while there was to help an Indian, by name "Rube," to build a log hut, receiving as pay five sacks of potatoes.

We had as a near neighbor J. N. Stevens, prominent in that country because he owned a store in Blackfoot and was also a Commissioner.

Mr. Stevens one day told me he intended to have some wood chopped down on the "bottoms" of Snake river and said he would take all I could chop at $2.00 per cord. Seeing in this an opportunity to at least make a living for my family I eagerly accepted the offer.

The snow was very deep in Idaho that winter, ten or twelve inches on the level; however, none fell in that vicinity to "lay on" until about the middle of January.

On account of the sparsely settled condition of the country every man went armed, not because there was any *real* danger, but there was much *imaginary* danger from Indians and wild beasts.

The timber on Snake river where I labored was about two miles from our house. Provided with rubber boots to wade through the deep snow, a Winchester rifle, a 45 Colt's revolver, and my dinner pail and ax I set out every morning just before day for the timber. I was young, strong and athletic and have never enjoyed a winter any more in my life.

The first three days of my wood chopping were industrious ones; I enjoyed the solitude of the woods, naturally supposing myself to be the only man on the river bottoms for many miles.

The fourth day of my new work found me doing some investigating; I thought to "look around" a little and study the locality. I had only gone down the river about a quarter of a mile, following an old channel, when I was greatly surprised to discover a small log cabin ensconsed in a cluster of willows. The rear of the cabin butted up against the bank so that it might be taken for the entrance to a tunnel mine.

Judging from the surroundings the occupant had not been there long; yet the cabin did not have a "new" appearance; again it did not seem old. From the side on which I approached I could see no window. My first impression was that it must be the entrance to a gravel mine. This thought, however, was dispelled when I discovered a small bit of chimney projecting above the rear roof. I thought I could discern a faint streak of blue smoke ascending from it. My first impression was one of disappointment: for had I not supposed myself to be the only person on the river that morning? The sun was shining brightly, there was not a cloud in the sky, the thermometer was 5 degrees below zero. I had felt within myself that I was nearer to God than I had ever been in all my life.

The little structure was so hidden by willows that not until I was within twenty feet of it had I discovered it; so my contemplation was at short range. A wash pan, turned bottom side up on a stump just outside the door, told me the cabin was occupied. Thinking to make the acquaintance of my new neighbor I approached the door.

A short strap hung through a hole that had been burned through the door. Just above the strap were two words characteristic of frontier life. They had been burnt into the door: "Come in." I pulled the strap, and as the door swung open the long, lean, gaunt figure of a man slowly arose from a rude bunk made of poles covered with cedar boughs, blankets and fur skins. There was hardly room enough for him to stand erect between the dirt floor and the ceiling. In a rather stooping attitude, with hands hanging limp by his side he faced me, and in smooth and mellow tones he said:

"Brother Pottenger, I believe? Good morning."

"That is my name," I replied; "but you have the best of me in knowing it; I do not remember ever having seen you before."

"What matters it? We are neighbors and ought to be friends," he said; at the same time he pointed to a chair before the fireplace.

This piece of furniture was so constructed as to do double duty, either as a chair in which to sleep or one on which to sit. He replenished the fire and, as I occupied the only chair in the house, sat on the floor with his back against the chimney. The side of his body next to the fire was very close to it; so close, in fact, that I momentarily thought his clothes would ignite. He did not seem to mind the heat in the least, notwithstanding I had to move my chair farther back in order to be comfortable.

He was glad of my company; this I saw and mentally resolved to learn all I could from him. With this object in view I began to question. What was his name? How long he had lived there? What was his business? And was he a miner or trapper? I had seen none of the working tools of either profession lying around, though I thought if he were the former he might be "laying off" for the day on account of the weather. He answered all my questions satisfactorily until I asked why the river upon whose pebbly bed we were then sitting was called the "Snake river." Immediately a new light shone in his black eyes. Taking a pebble from the mantel over the fireplace he handed it to me with the very surprising reply: "Read your answer in that and, if its language is foreign, then turn your eyes within."

I took the pebble and at once saw a beautiful specimen of the moss agate in which the Snake river abounds. But the mute pebble spoke not a word. I turned to my host with a questioning look.

"Man has within him the key to the process by which he may know all there is to know," he said, looking at me with his black penetrating eyes. I felt he had spoken a truth, the immensity of which I could not then comprehend. I felt, too, that those same words either

had befallen my ears once before or that they were to be repeated to me some time in the future. I felt they were big with prophesy and the truth.

Seeing my perplexity the stranger took the pebble and said, "I called you 'brother' when I addressed you a while ago because I recognize that the source of your life and mine are the same. Coming from the great city of Chicago—the acme of civilization—as you have recently, and now finding yourself in such surroundings as these I am not surprised that you should be astonished at finding a man of my appearance thus speaking to you; but, my brother, there is nothing strange in life; and there are no secrets in nature beyond man's ability to find out, because *he has within him the key to the process by which he may know all there is to know.*

"This pebble is a world.

"It is full of life.

"The source of its life is the same as that from which you and I draw our life.

"It will speak to us in its own language and tell us the history of this river, but in order to understand it one must be able to read the soul of things.

"It is a fractional part of the river.

"It is also a fractional part of this world and in that sense has for its source the same origin as your body and mine.

"This river's bed is made up of pebbles that seemingly lie so close together that there is no space between them, yet that space is filled with life, real living entities.

"This world of ours is only a pebble among other worlds—also pebbles—and the space between is not a vacuum only in so far as it contains no matter or earthy substance.

"The iron forming the beautiful tree you see in that crystal was once held in solution and was free; it is now held by atomic attraction in that form. It has its counterpart in millions of pebbles and the tree you see pictured there is the image of trees on other worlds.

"As the body of the individual is the medium, or vehicle, through which the individual mind or spirit expresses itself, so the universe in its entirety is the body or medium through which the universal mind or spirit of God finds expression.

"By universe is meant not only the world upon which we live, but the sun and the entire starry heavens.

"As there are organs in the physical body having a special purpose, so there are worlds and systems of worlds in the great universal body performing special duties. Indeed, planetary systems have their special molecular construction the same as special organs and parts of our bodies have particular atomic and molecular make-up. For instance, the atomic and molecular construction of the planet Mars is no more similar to that of Saturn than the atomic and molecular construction of the heart is similar to that of the liver. The heart could not perform its function of contraction and dilation if it were composed of the material of which the liver is made. The atoms of matter that enter into the composition of the bones of our bodies could not possibly do duty as a part of the eye. The vibrations of the atoms of which the bones are composed are too low. A collection of bone atoms in the eye would soon cause ossification of that organ.

"The spirit or mind of man acts through *all* of the parts and members and organs of which his body is composed. He is glorified in and through them. As they respond to his will he is *joyful*.

"Worlds and systems of worlds are only atoms compared to the universe of infinity.

"This world of ours, while appearing large to us mortals, is only an atom in the grand make-up of the universe; only one of a cluster that forms a group, and this group has its place and function to perform in the great universal whole the same as the heart has a function in our bodies.

"Worlds, suns and systems have their individual personalities and consequent influences, just the same as human beings have their personal and individual influences among their kind.

"That which we can comprehend with our physical senses, such as seeing, feeling, etc., may be called the physical universe. We can see the sun, moon and stars with our natural eyes because our physical eyes can record the vibrations of light emanating from those bodies. We can see, feel and touch the physical bodies of our fellow being because our bodies can record the vibrations emanating from their bodies.

"Their bodies and ours are made up of the same materials as the planetary bodies. The materials of which our bodies are made must forever remain with the planet, that is to say, we cannot take from one planet to another our physical bodies any more than the heart can incorporate within itself the atoms of matter belonging to the liver, as the life principle in the atoms composing the liver would not permit them to respond to the life principle of the heart.

"In fact, disease is the result of the unnatural incorporation of atoms into portions of the body where they do not belong and for which they are not specially fitted, by education or drill, through long and successive experiences in the worlds of mineral, vegetable and animal.

"There is not a bone, muscle, tendon, fiber or organ in the human body but has its counterpart millions of times in the kingdoms below man.

"There is not an atom of matter in man's physical body but is teeming with life; and if it could be seen by our natural eyes it would be discerned to be radiating a light, and at some place in the starry expanse of the universe there is a sun, the light from which exactly corresponds with the light in that atom.

"Matter, then, is intercepted light and man's physical body becomes a battleground for the elements of matter.

"So long as man's soul, mind or spirit can govern his body, or so long as his will or intelligence can keep life in it, just so long can man have mastery over so-called death, evil and sin.

"This world of ours is now rushing through space at the rate of about 60,000 miles per hour. A railroad train speeding over the country at 60 miles per hour is in our estimation a wonder; with its jingling and jarring it soon shakes itself to pieces, but its speed is nothing compared to that of the earth; yet we have mentioned only one motion of the earth, that of its forward motion around the sun. There are many other motions belonging to it, such as its oscillating, back and forth motion or vibration, then its axial vibration. Everything of which the earth is composed has all these vibrations; the granite, porphyry, sandstone, slate, coal, marble—all have this general vibration belonging to the earth; then in addition to the general vibration of the earth they have their own individual life.

"Each stratum of the earth's crust emitting a different light; each and every metal singing a different song.

"Visit your rolling mills and smelters and watch the process of raising the vibrations of these metals and minerals and stones.

"See how, by the application of heat their atomic construction is changed, and the ray of light that was intercepted millions and milllions of years ago becomes liberated and that which at one moment is cold matter, passes from the crystal to the molten condition, then from the molten by the application of more heat, into the gaseous or ethereal state. It is now no longer visible. The life that was imprisoned has been set free. We do not see it because our eyes do not record its vibrations.

"Man's physical body is a machine recording the vibrations emanating from the sun, moon and other planetary bodies. Not so, however, his mind or spiritual body.

"No one will deny to man a mind, yet we cannot with our physical senses see it. We cannot handle it.

"We know man thinks, yet we cannot see his thoughts nor weigh them.

"We know man has a spirit and a will, yet it is beyond his power to confine the will or circumscribe the spirit.

"Man's physical body is a reflection of his mental or spiritual body, and just so the physical universe, including the sun and the starry heavens; they too are a reflection of a spiritual or mental universe. Just as real from the standpoint of mind as the material universe is real from the standpoint of matter.

"The mortal man cannot record the vibrations of the mental world except through the process of so-called thinking. He cannot see the mental world with his natural eyes. If he could he would see with his natural eyes the minds of men, and language of any known means would be unnecessary. Deception would then be impossible.

"Man's spiritual or mental body is his polar opposite—his other self—living in a mental universe whose mental worlds, suns and systems of suns are as natural as ours.

"This other self constitutes man's ideals.

"Every man has his ideal woman.

"Every woman has her ideal man.

"Being unable, however, to make the divine union or marriage (a union of the lower nature with the higher, which simply means to recognize one's own conscience,) they take a substitute, and the *union intended* really becomes a separation as the substitute proves to be more attractive than the real higher self, or in other words, the substitute may prove a stumbling block to soul growth.

"Then again the substitute may be a light bearer, and a help, a true savior to an erring soul. How often in the affairs of man do we see men and women forgiving the most heinous crimes in each other, and yet neither one is the ideal of the other—only a substitute.

"Marriage then becomes a symbol of a universal law.

"It tells us in symbolic language that man has a spiritual nature; that his own spirit is his bride. That his bride is just as beautiful as his thoughts are beautiful. That she is just as pure and virtuous as his thoughts are pure and virtuous.

"That she is a song bird, or an artist, as he wills her to be.

"As he cultivates her acquaintance he soon learns that without her he can do nothing. She enters into all his joys and his sorrows. He talks to her in solitude and she speaks to him on the mountain top. She applauds him in deeds of valor and makes him feel the kiss of angels when relieving distress. She goes with him into the courts of justice and pleads for the erring. When man sins against his fellow man she turns her face and weeps, but she does not desert him. She protests against every sin before it is committed and while not forgiving, she never runs away.

"Seeing and knowing her *substitute* she makes no objection because she is happy in being the *spiritual mother to his children.*"

During the delivery of this metaphysical lecture I had sat in respectful silence trying to determine in my own mind the sanity or insanity of the strange man before me.

He had every appearance of being a perfectly normal man, yet there was an air about him of superiority, a something that caused one to feel intellectually pygmean beside this man who, by his conversation, was proving himself to be a superior sort of personage.

Thinking, however, that after all he might only be expressing the vagaries of a diseased mind I thought to test his sanity by asking a few questions.

He seemed to have anticipated my mental attitude; he had stopped in his discourse and, now standing as nearly erect as he could, because of the low ceil, was eyeing me as though he would search my very soul.

"You speak of other worlds, suns, and systems with a great familiarity," I said; "perhaps you can tell me something of the life and customs of the inhabitants of those orbs?" I had asked the question thinking that if he claimed for them a human occupation I would know for a surety he was crazy.

"I should be pleased to tell you of the life on other worlds but you would only call me insane and there would be no profit in such conversation."

I again felt the force of his truthful words and arose to take my departure, but he gently yet firmly pushed me back into the chair, saying, as he did so, "It's a cold day outside and, as you seem to have an open mind, I wish to plant therein a few truths which may lie dormant for many years but at the proper time and place you will give them rightful birth and in such manner as will do the world good.

"You asked about other worlds a moment ago and I presume you, in common with all humanity, think that this world is the only one inhabited? If so, disabuse your mind of the illusion, for among other worlds this one (terra) is known as the planet of Selfishness and Sorrow. You have but to consider the motives that prompt humanity in anything it does to see the truth in my statement.

"Every act of every human being is a selfish one.

"A man educates his children in order that they may be an honor to the family name.

"A loving mother rushes through the burning home to save her babe because of her love for it, rather than its love for her.

"Every sacrifice made by one human in the interest of another when reduced to the primitive motive is found to be selfish.

"Analyze the love you bear for your wife and you will discover it to be jealousy, for if you really love her and desire her happiness above your own you will permit her perfect freedom in loving and doing as she pleases, and it matters not what she does, nor whom, nor what she loves.

"Sorrow is another inherent principle belonging to this planet; it comes to every one and to everything. None can escape the tear of sorrow.

"There are other worlds where the inhabitants do not know what sorrow, nor pain, nor discord means.

"They do not ravish nature in any way by cutting down trees to make their homes, as their houses simply *grow into existence* from such materials as the thinker desires his home to be made of. It is furnished according to his thought and when the owner no longer has use for it he simply lets go of it, in thought, and the materials go back to their original elements—disappear, vanish.

"Ask one of those people to take the life of an animal and they would not know how to go about the task. They do not know how to kill for the reason that they have no idea of death.

"In order to kill one must believe in death; one must have a knowledge of death. One must have hatred in his heart, and above all one must be able to express death.

"They could put life into an inanimate body if it were necessary, because they understand the *source of life* and its manifestations.

"Upon this old world the people know how to *take* life but they have no conception of how to give it.

"Every human being, at heart, is a murderer, for he believes in death, not only to his fellow animal, but believes in death to himself.

"If I ask you to give life to a rabbit you are powerless, but if I ask you to take its life you know the process.

"By what right or statute has man to take what he cannot give?

"The history of the world is one long record of death."

I interrupted my host at this point to ask if he believed that the works of God were perfect and therefore good? To this he replied with new enthusiasm, "Most assuredly all things are good and of God. This planet is expressing itself perfectly and as a planet fulfilling its every purpose.

"The highest intelligence possible to be evolved from a cheese is a maggot.

"The greatest possibilities within a hen egg is a chick.

"The greatest specimen of evolved intelligence on earth to-day is the human animal. It represents the acme of the earth's labors and power. Among principles this world expresses death and it cannot express anything else.

"The object and purpose, then, of this earth is to afford souls an opportunity to *meet and overcome death*.

"The general of an army was once a member of the awkward squad.

"He can perform the duties of all the officers from corporal of the guard to commander-in-chief, because he has filled those offices and responded to the life force of the position. He has been identified with every step from the lowest to the highest and as commander-in-chief he includes within himself the entire army.

"Look at the great army of humanity peopling the earth and answer why there should be such vast differences in intellectual and soul growth. Consider the dense ignorance of those people at the North Pole, in Africa, Australia and many other parts of the world, and compare them with the intellectual power and soul growth of such nations as the German, French, English and American."

My host then picked up a joint of stove pipe lying on the floor, which had theretofore escaped my notice, and standing it on end thus addressed me:

"Suppose you imagine several small tubes attached to the bottom of this stove pipe and suppose you imagine further that each of the tubes be filled with a different colored chalk. Then if pure crystal water be turned into the stove pipe it would escape out of the tubes and be many colored according to the lining of the tube?

"It is the same water that flows through all.

"So it is with the planets of this universe. They each receive the same sunshine but each reflects that life according to its nature.

"Planets, of themselves, without living entities upon them, have practically no influence.

"Hate has no power except there be an instrument through which it may work.

"Love must have a medium or she starves to death. Give her an opportunity and she will people the earth.

"Every moral, ethical and criminal law has for its source the same fount.

"The love in the tiger's heart that prompts it to feed its young on the warm blood of the fawn is the same love that leads the Indian woman on to the burning pile of her dead husband.

"Schools, colleges, seminaries, prisons and penal institutions of all kinds, the church, the poorhouse, the insane asylum, all are filled with the same love. The saint and the sinner had an equal start and both will reach the same goal.

"Every human soul is a reflector of Divine love. Every world is a radiator (by the medium of the life upon it) of the same energy."

I interrupted again to ask a question, thinking my newly made acquaintance was getting tired and would probably sit down, and then we could talk of mundane affairs. I also surmised that the nature of my question would preclude the possibility of any extended remarks, as it might be answered by a simple yes or no. I also said to him that it would be my last question as I was anxious to be going; besides I wanted to get by myself so I could think over and analyze what I had heard.

"Is it possible for human beings to go consciously from one planet to another?" I asked.

For a moment he hung his head as if in deep thought, then he stepped forward, laid a hand on each of my shoulders and looked me long and steadily in the eye. During the process I felt as if I were being reviewed for centuries back. It seemed to me as if he had gotten hold of my thread of life and was following it to the end of time. Then he stepped back, turned his face from me and took an attitude of supplication and prayer without kneeling. In a few moments he turned to me and his whole manner had changed and I saw that he felt a deep sense of responsibility. My question had such an effect upon him that I almost wished I could have withdrawn it. Finally he turned and said:

"Do you read the Bible and are you familiar with the Ten Commandments?"

'I do and I am," I replied.

"Then you know that one of them says, 'Take not the name of the Lord thy God in vain.'

"I do," I said.

"You also know that the Bible says, 'Swear not at all'?" Again I answered in the affirmative.

"I am going to answer your question regarding interplanetary intercourse, but before doing so I want to explain the true meaning of those two quotations. There are those in the world who, by reason of their calling, such as the teacher, metaphysician, the priest, the preacher, the medical doctor, gain the confidence of their fellow man on the ground that they are doing God's work in the eradication of disease, sin and ignorance. They claim a Divine right to know your inmost thoughts and demand that you subjugate your physical bodies to them.

"Humanity believes in these professions and the statute books are full of laws made in their interest.

"Any one who uses the name of the Lord to further his own interests, or who uses this confidence for any other purpose than for good is taking the name of the Lord in vain; that is to say, he is using God's power which is the power of faith and love, for no good purpose and is therefore diverting it from its true course.

"He who takes an oath or obligation is bound and is not free to serve God whenever he may find him. He who is bound by oath to church creed or dogma is limited in his investigations and cannot recognize humanity as his brother because of this obligation.

"Therefore if you would be free 'swear not at all.'

"I find upon investigation that so far you have taken no obligations that will interfere with your giving to the world such knowledge as may be acquired by you during the course of your sojourn here and it is not likely that you ever will."

The suggestive remarks called to my mind a conversation I had overheard when I was a very small boy between my father and a brother Mason regarding the probable disposition of Captain William Morgan, whose supposed expose of Masonry in 1826 was the cause of a new political party at that time. My interesting friend (for so I had now cause to regard him) seemingly read my mind for he said:

"Morgan was never drowned. The teaching of Masonry is that of charity, brotherly love, forgiveness. Masonry has never yet created the office of executioner. She has never taught revenge. She does not claim eye for eye, tooth for tooth.

"There are men who cannot recognize humanity as one grand brotherhood, therefore, it is necessary to place some sort of restriction upon them.

"Fear is the best weapon to hold in check man's animal nature, so the church holds over the heads of its votaries the fear of eternal punishment in order to make them good. Were it not for this fear and hold the church has, crime would run rampant in the world.

"Masonry imposes the most sacred obligation given under such conditions as to fill the breast of the candidate with fear everlasting should he even think of divulging its secrets. It gives a scientific reason for the practice of charity; it demonstrates why we should love one another; and by mathematics alone, if by no other means, it proves its right as a teacher to mankind.

"Why should a man be sworn and obligated to love his fellow man?

"Why should a man find it necessary to take oath in order to forgive a wrong or practice charity?

"Why should a man feel that in order to know the secrets of the stars and his own soul it is necessary to be obligated?

"The church says, 'There is a tree; there is a man; there is a bird. God made the tree; He made the man and the bird; His ways are past finding out. Blessed be God.'

"The church places God afar off and tells man to find him. Masonry says, 'There is a tree; there is a man; there is a bird.' Then Masonry goes to work and ultimately, by the law of synthesis and demonstrable facts, tells *why* the tree is *not* a man, and why the man is *not* a bird.

"The church requires faith only.

"Masonry demands faith, but advises that to faith be added knowledge, reason. It admonishes its devotees of the fearfully close proximity of God, rather than his remoteness.

"The church removes from the individual the responsibility of sin, and allows him to elect a substitute to expiate his crimes.

"Masonry explains how impossible it is to escape the just punishment of every impure thought, unkind act or unholy impulse. She shows the law of God to the individual and proves to man that he is his own creator, his own preserver, his own destroyer.

"The church permits a man to live a life of crime and allows him salvation at the grave.

"Masonry teaches that the crime becomes a debt and accumulates interest, by Karmic law, to be paid in suffering of its kind.

"The church lives in and deals with time only. Masonry, by her symbols, teaches that time is a factor of matter and that the present is eternity."

I was intensely interested in the argument of the man before me, although I knew nothing of Masonry. I was, or rather had been, a member of the Baptist Church; I had always found it impossible to harmonize all the teachings of the church. I could not bring myself to believe that God could or would create an adversary superior in power to himself, as it seemed to me his Satanic Majesty was.

His references to Masonry were most pleasing, for my first impressions in life were of my father's Masonic Apron and Sash; how I used to steal into his private office and, taking the beautiful Apron from its hiding place, I would tie the strings around my body just under the arms and stand in front of the large mirror, first with the Apron on and then the Sash. If I put them both on at the same time, the Sash covered up too much of the Apron.

I recalled the admiration with which I, as a child, had studied and wondered what all those beautiful pictures meant. The All-Seeing Eye, the Square and Compass, the letter G, the two Columns surmounted with the Globes, the Ladder, the Tiled Floor, the Starry Heavens and Clouds; and then the peculiar construction of the Apron also attracted my young mind, and I wondered why there was a three cornered flap.

The lodge room was only a few blocks from our house and was over a grocery store. I recalled how I used to coax my elder brother to take me down by the lodge room so I could hear the Masons sing. My respect for Masonry, therefore, was more than is carried by the average person, and I was ravishingly hungry for any light that might be given me regarding my early questionings.

Judging by his manner and conversation that he must be a member of the craft, and still thinking there might be a soft spot in his brain, I secretly resolved to question him and perhaps through the "soft spot" some "inside" information might be gained. I had read in my father's old "Masonic Review" so much about "the word" that I wanted light on that subject particularly. Recalling the old saying, "Fools and children tell the truth," I fixed my eyes upon his and with a rather daring tone and inflection to my voice I asked: "Are you a Mason?"

"I am," he replied.

He did not volunteer any further information and I was at a loss to know how further to proceed. Growing desperate I asked with perhaps more of the challenge in my voice than in the previous question,

"What is a Mason?"

"A builder."

"A builder of what?" said I.

"A temple," he replied.

Then recalling the practice of laying corner stones and dedicatory services I again asked:

"To whom is the temple dedicated?"

"To the living God," he answered softly and with reverence.

"Whence does the Mason get his materials?"

"From the Universe."

"Why cannot we distinguish a Masonic temple from other buildings?"

"Because all architecture is Masonic and there can be no distinction."

I realized I was not getting what I wanted. I had expected my newly formed acquaintance only needed a start and he would unwind but he seemed to be economical of words all at once and I again sought light by asking:

"I understand that in Masonry there is a word, the possession of which brings great power?"

"Yes."

"Have you the word?" I asked.

"I have," he answered.

I felt now that I had gotten to the fountain I was searching for: I also felt that I had only to ask this peculiar man the vital question and then I should be in possession of that which I had for so many years longed; still there was a guilty conscience within me that told me I would better get the word or information I sought in the same manned my friend had obtained it. I felt I had not earned what I was asking. It seemed to me that I should like to retrace but, having started, I persisted by asking,

"Will you give it to me?"

"You have it," he said.

"You lie," I said, quick as a flash, and oh, how I did wish I could have recalled those words; but they were out and said before I knew it. Then he turned questioner.

"Did you ever speak the universal, eternal truth?"

"I believe I have on a few occasions."

"Mention one."

"I said to my wife this morning that I would be at home for supper."

"That is not true. Give me another instance."

His reply frightened me, for there was but one thing that would prevent my eating supper that night with my family and that was death, and I began to speculate how I could make my words true, and him a liar. My desire for "light" was now about gone, and my conviction sure that this man was crazy and fully intended to do me harm. Seeing my discomfiture he smiled and said:

"Come, give me another instance of when you spoke the eternal truth."

"My father years ago asked me just before retiring one night 'if I had slopped the hogs,' and as it was my daily work and I recall the circumstances now, I am positive I did slop the hogs that particular evening, and I am also quite positive that I spoke the truth when answering him."

With a merry twinkle in his eye he replied. "And I can with equal truth tell you, that you lie. Now brother Pottenger let me explain a little the enigma into which we seem to have gotten. You will eat supper with your family to-night. You did swill the pigs, but your actions there and your acts to-night were for *time* and not for eternity. If you should return to your old homestead you, no doubt, would find the scene changed.

"The pigs have disappeared; the old stable and pig-pen have perhaps given way to newer buildings; the family that gathered around the hearth that night have been dispersed, and never again during the ilfe of the world can the same conditions be reproduced as existed at that time. No picture of your surroundings that evening would be perfect except it contain all the factors to the minutest detail. Do you think it possible to again reproduce the circumstance of that evening?"

"I do not," I replied.

"Do you think that what you eat at supper to-night and the process of eating and the surroundings of the meal will eternally exist?"

"I do not," I answered; "and I am not yet convinced that I have not spoken the truth in the two instances referred to."

"Yes," he said; "you have spoken the *relative* truth but not the *eternal* truth. The chair you sit in is changeable. It is destructible and therefore is not eternal. The mental picture of the chair will remain in the mental atmosphere of the world long after the chair ceases to be, just the same as you can now recall the circumstances of the evening when your father asked you the question regarding the pigs.

"There is a mental or spiritual atmosphere of the world just the same as there is a material atmosphere.

"The mental atmosphere extends away from the earth and reaches to the mental atmosphere of other worlds, thus making it possible for communion between worlds but the interchange is mental and not physical.

"There," he said, pointing to a broken plate lying on a box, "is a spoonful or so of black sand (and he took a small horse shoe magnet from his vest pocket); "take this magnet, hold it underneath the plate and you will see it influence those particles as though they had life."

I did as bidden and found he was correct; that the magnet did cause the particles to move. I was surprised at this for I had supposed that china and glassware were non-conductors. He noticed my surprise and said:

"If the plate were wood, cork, India rubber, isinglass, in fact, any non-conducting substance for *electricity*, the *magnet* would influence them just the same; and if magnetism can pass through and between the particles composing that plate without disturbing their molecular construction, what, in your opinion, would be able to stop thought? and yet thought is a coarse material substance compared with soul.

"I shall not attempt at this time to inform you of the difference between matter, spirit, and soul, but sufficient to say that soul only is eternal; and he who can unite spirit, soul and body, and then speak or act from the standpoint of soul, whatsoever he doeth is done for eternity, and whatsoever he sayeth is not only true but it is eternally true."

Lowering his voice and pointing his finger at me in a sort of bantering manner he asked,

"How would you like to be able to speak and express eternal truth the rest of your life?"

"Nothing would afford me more pleasure," I replied.

Immediately his whole frame seemed filled with a new fire and the atmosphere of the cabin became stifling as he fairly hissed through his teeth,—"Then you would be the most dangerous and destructive man in the world. If you had the power to speak eternal truth and you should say to a man 'be damned' he would be damned throughout eternity and there would be no changing his condition.

"If you should say to a sick person 'be thou made whole or clean,' he would immediately recover and his recovery would be permanent.

"If you had the power to speak truth from the standpoint of soul you could command the world to dissolve and immediately it would disappear. Truth is a most fearful and powerful weapon. He who would express truth assumes a most stupendous responsibility. With your human passions and desires, if you had the power to speak the truth you could command nations to be annihilated. You could command the sun, the moon and stars."

I interrupted the speaker at this point to ask the following question,—

"You say there is a mental atmosphere; please tell me what you mean?"

"Just what I say, and that mental atmosphere is filled with forms just the same as the world of matter is filled with material forms. All forms exist first in mind, then in matter, and when the material form is destroyed the mental form still lives.

"Principles take form and present themselves to the human mind in the shape of symbols."

"Do you mean to tell me," I said, "that if I should write a book, or an essay, I would simply be externalizing that which already exists in the universal mind?"

"You have it," he replied. "We all have two minds, one the mundane or imperfect mind, the other the celestial or perfect mind.

"One knows in part, the other knows all, and as the perfect or celestial mind penetrates and interpenetrates the world of matter without its presence being known (to the latter), just the same as you saw the magnetism penetrate the dish without disturbing the atoms of its construction, so the soul is present in a still more attenuated form and equally unknown to both mind and matter. The earth is a huge magnet with two magnetic poles, but there are many nodal points or magnetic centers which cause the ocean currents and other phenomena of nature. Cities, towns and hamlets are magnetic centers on the mental plane and there are highways of thought between these cities just the same as there are ocean currents connecting one point of land with another.

"The earth is one great ball of quivering life. The strata and seams of metal in the earth are its veins and arteries.

"Telephone, electric and cable wires are grand highways for the spirit of fire to travel from point to point and find expression through human brain. The spirit of fire is known among the ancients as 'Salamander.' Fire is life to it as meat and potatoes are to you."

Again I interrupted my host to ask a question, feeling sure, however, that if he were a sane man on most subjects he certainly was insane to believe that fire could be food or life under any circumstances, for so far in life I had never known of fire to be anything but an agent of destruction, and to change the trend of his thought I essayed to ask the following question:

"You remarked awhile ago that 'matter was intercepted light and that man's physical body was a battleground for the elements of matter.' I will be obliged if you will explain that statement."

"Your question is in line with the subject I was just treating," and as if my question had not broken in upon his trend of thought at all he proceeded:

"The sun is the source of all life. Fire is nothing but liberated sunshine; the tree locks up the sunshine in its cells; then when that sunshine is liberated heat is the result.

"If you apply heat to water you liberate the sunshine and it is called *steam*, and as such is a powerful agent. Salt will not burn; it is therefore watery and will assume a liquid condition. It will not freeze and is therefore fiery.

"It is by nature a crystal and is therefore earthy.

"Salt may be said to contain the three elements of fire, water and earth. It is the neuter element in which the two polar opposites, fire and water, unite.

" 'Undine' is the name of the spirit of water; 'Salamander' is the name of the spirit of fire; 'Gnome' is the name of the spirit of earth.

"Man's physical body has heat (fire), moisture (water), salt (earth), and wherever these elements are there may be found also the life or spirit of those elements; and as fire and water are bitter enemies, forever striving to exterminate each other, you can readily see how man's physical body is a battleground for the warring elements of nature.

"Were it not for salt fire would consume the earth. Were it not for water, salt would crystallize everything into its steely embrace and there would be no life. Were it not for the presence of fire, salt and water would lie down together and never express life.

"Eternal rest would be the result.

"The foundation of Masonry is the infinite North, East, West and

South. The materials of which her temple is builded are the eternal elements, fire, earth, air and water, and the Mason himself is the soul of the universe. He is not limited in his expression to one planet, nor to one system of planets, but during the early stages of soul-growth progress may be slow and limited to the narrow confines of one solar system.

"You cannot take your physical body from this planet, because it is a part of the planet and the world needs every atom belonging to it. You can, however, go in thought or spirit to other worlds.

"It is not a profitable thing to attempt, however, to visit other worlds alone; under the tutorship of an experienced soul it may be accomplished, but not without its attending dangers at all times.

"There are souls whose knowledge of vibratory law permits them to express themselves on the different worlds. When the conditions require an extraordinary impetus, when there is a great work to be done, a master equal to the occasion appears. The nature of the work will determine the nature of the appearance.

"Sometimes a master has but a single message to give, and he gives it to the open receptive mind of a boy in the field through the medium of a flower that attracts the youngster's attention as he stops in his play to ask the flower the source of its color.

"If it be necessary, an interplanetary soul may take on the physical form, appear in a neighborhood, and for a time take an active interest in the affairs of that locality, then, when its work has been accomplished, disappear as unannounced as it made its appearance.

"But in order to build a body and clothe it, the soul must be a master in fact of the elements composing that world. It must be able to attract in due form and regular order the materials necessary for its natural manifestation among men.

"The metals and crystals of earth would have no special attraction for such a soul, for having the power to control gold by his will he would not wrong a fellow human for the possession of it.

"Being united within itself and sexless, all humanity would receive the same kindly feeling from such a soul; every woman a sister, every man a brother.

"The medium by which information is carried from one planet to another is soul, and as there is in the soul realm no diversity of tongues, the knowledge that is transferred from one planet to another must be by means of symbols. You are a symbol and *you have within you the key to the process by which you may know all there is to know.*"

"Jumping to my feet I exclaimed, "If what you say is true then it is provable."

"Yes," he said, "prove the truth or falsity of what I have said by making a personal application of every symbol presented to you.

"Ask yourself what there is in you to correspond to the symbol.

"Nature works in purpose, not in vain."

I bade my new found neighbor a hearty good evening, for the day was about spent. I said not a word to any one of the strange man on the river bottom and a few days afterward, feeling that I had a little spare time, I thought I would call on my neighbor, so I again sought his abode, but to my utter surprise and disappointment I could not again find the location of the cabin, nor could I find any tracks in the snow showing where any one had come into the timber or gone out. All that winter I went daily to the woods and frequently took little hunting excursions through that portion of the river bottom where the cabin had stood but I never found any trace of my man.

I was young and ambitious, the future then seemed bright to me, and my mind was filled with earthly affairs rather than occultism; gradually the incident of the strange man in the cabin became simply a pleasant memory.

DIVINE TRUTH

CHAPTER II.

A Search for Truth—To Know Truth One Must Be Truth—
What a Symbol Is—How the Ancients by Means of Sym-
bols Have Perpetuated Their Knowledge of Universal
Laws—The Church, Freemasonry and the People Each
Entrusted With a Duty—Only the People Have Been
True to the Charge—The Bible of the Ancients Is To-
Day a Plaything and Known as a Pack of Playing Cards
—The Discovery of America and Development of the
United States Precludes the Necessity of Longer Keep-
ing Secret the Real True Nature of This Sacred Book of
Symbols—Beauty of Symbolism.

The above Masonic symbol is a pictorial reproduction of the signet worn by King Solomon.

One of several interpretations is: "I search for divine truth."

With this as our motto we begin these pages, and invite the reader to peruse this book.

Truth has no authority, no substitutes. In order to fully comprehend Truth we must become that Truth.

We may *apprehend* the duties of a king or a president; to fully *comprehend* them we must fill the office.

We may *apprehend* the remorse of a felon in his cell; to fully *comprehend* it we must have committed his crime and have suffered his conviction.

We may *apprehend* the advantages and disadvantages of being rich; in order to *comprehend* we must be rich.

A symbol is not the thing symbolized, but needs interpretation.

A symbol is a substitute for the thing behind it.

Paphus, one of the many great mystics of the past, declared that just before the world was plunged into that wonderful mental and spiritual abyss, known as the Dark Ages, there were three universal methods employed for the transmission of wisdom from one generation to another. Those old sages knew that the world was about to enter upon an epoch of sensuality of such magnitude that fraternity and fellowship would be almost, if not entirely, obliterated. They knew of the triune nature of man, that he possesses a spiritual body, and that it is governed by fixed spiritual laws. I quote from the "Tarot of the Bohemians," by Paphus translated from the French by A. P. Morton and published in 1896 in London by George Redway:

Analysis has been carried in every branch of knowledge as far as possible and has only deepened the moats which divide the sciences.

Synthesis becomes necessary; but how can we realize it? But the use of synthesis had been almost entirely lost. Among the ancients knowledge was only transmitted to men whose worth had been proven by a series of tests. [The same conditions are supposed to prevail today.] This transmission took place in the temples under the name of *Mysteries*, and the adept assumed the title of *Priest* or *Initiate*. However, when the Initiate found that a time was approaching when these doctrines might be lost to humanity he made strenuous efforts to save the Law of Synthesis from oblivion. Three methods were employed:

1. Secret societies; a direct continuation of the mysteries.

2. The Cultus; a symbolic translation of the higher doctrines for the use of the people.

3. And last, the people themselves became the unconscious depository of the doctrine.

The Arabs, Alchemists, Templars, Rosicrucians and Freemasons form the western chain in the transmission of occult science. A rapid glance over the doctrines of these associations is sufficient to prove that the present form of Freemasonry has almost entirely lost the meanings of the traditional symbols, which constitute the trust it should have transmitted through the ages.

The elaborate ceremonials of the ritual appear ridiculous to the vulgar common sense of a lawyer or grocer, the actual modern representatives of the profound doctrines of antiquity. In fact, Freemasonry has lost the doctrine confided to it, and cannot, of itself, supply us with the Synthetic Law for which we are seeking. The task of the religious sects was the development of the philosophical and metaphysical aspects of the doctrine. Every priest of an ancient creed was one of the initiates; he was fully aware that but one religion existed, and that the Cultus merely served to translate this religion to the different nations according to their different temperaments.

The Christian and the Mussulman were the cause of the total loss of the secret doctrine which gave the key to Synthetic Unity.

The Jews alone possessed no longer the spirit but only the letter of their oral or Kabalistic traditions. The Bible written in Hebrew is marvelous; it contains all the occult traditions, although its true sense has never yet been revealed. Every cultus has its tradition, its book, its bible. These teach those who know how to read them the unity of all creeds, despite the difference existing in the rituals of various countries. To him possessing the key, all bibles reveal the same doctrine. It is useless, however, to search for this doctrine among the western creeds. The sages suffered no illusions respecting the possible future of the tradition which they confided to the intelligence and virtue of future generations. Moses had chosen a people to hand down through succeeding ages the book which contained all the science of Egypt; but even before Moses, the Hindu Initiates had selected a nation to hand down to future generations the primitive doctrines of the great civilizations of the Atlantides.

The people have never disappointed the expectations of those who trusted it. Understanding none of the truths entrusted to them they carefully abstained from altering them in any way, and treated the slightest attack upon them as sacrilege. Thus, the Jews have transmitted to us intact the letters forming the cipher of Moses.

It was a great thing to give the people a book which they could adore, respectfully, and always guard intact, but to give them a book by means of which they would be enabled to live was yet better.

The people entrusted with the transmission of occult doctrines from the earliest ages were those of the Bohemian or Gypsy race.

THE GYPSIES.

The Gypsies possess a bible which has proved their means of gaining a livelihood, for it enables them to tell fortunes; furthermore it has been a perpetual source of amusement, for it enables them to gamble. Yes; the game of cards called the Tarot which the Gypsies possess is the Bible of Bibles. It is the book of Thoth Hermes Trismegistus, the book of Adam, the book of the primitive revelation of ancient civilization. Thus while the Freemason, an intelligent and virtuous man, has lost the tradition; while the priest, also intelligent and virtuous, has lost his esoterism, the Gypsy, despite both ignorance and viciousness, has given us the key which enables us to explain all the symbolism of the ages.

We must admire the wisdom of those Initiates who utilized vice and made it produce more beneficial results than virtue. The Gypsy pack of cards is a wonderful book. This pack, under the name of Tarot, Thora, Rota has formed the basis of the synthetic teachings of all the ancient nations successively. In it, where a man of the people sees only a means of amusement, the thinker will find the key to an obscure tradition. Louis Claude de St. Martin, the Unknown Philosopher, finds written in it the 'mysterious links which unite God, the universe, and man'.

It is not the purpose of the writer to show how by easy and natural stages that old and "scientific religion of the stars," known to and practised by the Atlantians, degenerated into the hundreds of cults and isms, (including Sun Worship and the great Phallic religion), practiced, it seems, in almost all parts of the earth.

It is not difficult to see why the church and the secret orders should lose their virtue. We have but to consider the selfishness, fear and ignorance of mankind to receive an answer. Spiritual, as well as material progress, moves in cycles and waves. Centuries of time are required, in many instances, for the return and fruition of a single law. It was necessary that spirituality sink to its lowest ebb that it should rise to the highest pinnacle in another direction. But before the Priest lost his virtue and the Mason his wisdom, the eternal truths of the universe were anchored on earth, and the chain has never been broken.

*   *   *   *   *   *

With the discovery of the Western Continent and the birth of the United States there disappeared further necessity for withholding the truth from mankind. The pendulum of truth, fraternity and virtue is swinging toward the other extreme, Truth regarding Nature's laws and those laws of man's own salvation is being slowly but surely revealed to him. It may cost the lives and existence of nations, but the law of the Lord is perfect and will be fulfilled.

The sacred trust and power confided to the church and fraternities have been shamefully abused; under pretense of giving religion and knowledge the people have been intentionally misled, but nature will right all her wrongs.

Previous to the establishment of the United States there was no country where man could worship God according to the dictates of his own conscience. All public learning and knowledge was colored and twisted to suit the purposes of the politician and priest. The politician, working through fraternal orders, determined the destiny of the nation. His chief ally has ever been the people's spiritual adviser. Indeed, these two have always worked hand in hand; not, indeed, for the dissemination of truth, but to conceal it. They knew full well that when wisdom and virtue filled office and directed the affairs of man they would be forced to abdicate. Knowing their claims to virtue and knowledge were false they would not and could not unmask themselves. Not having the truth they could not reveal it.

The office and power of politician and priest depended upon the ignorance and credulity of the people; hence, to keep the people in ignorance, *substitute* knowledge was given. It was the work of the Priest or spiritual teacher to keep the people in ignorance while the Politician levied assessments, collected taxes and administered affairs of government. Of course, governmental affairs were administered first in the interest of the politician, and then the church.

Between these two the people have been prevented from knowing the truth. If, by the operations of the Laws of God and the universe, a soul should be born which knew the truth and had the courage to express it, they cried with one voice: *"Crucify him, crucify him."*

Whenever a soul has ventured into the realm of truth and has dared make known his discoveries, the earth seemingly has opened and swallowed him. Even the great Swedenborg was obliged to abbreviate his descriptions, although he is contemporary with the present.

BEAUTY OF SYMBOLISM.

All nature is one vast symbol, a sort of kindergarten into which the soul of man is projected to make his own observations, and to study himself as he may see himself reflected through Nature's mirror.

The word hypocrite has been handed down to us from that remote past when religion was taught by means of theatrical troupes;
the actors not being allowed to appear in public unless wearing robes
and masks with which to conceal their identity. They were called
hypocrites, signifying "not what they appear to be." The priestly
robes of to-day, may they not be a remnant of that age?

The title "father" as applied to the priesthood had its origin
among a people who practiced the Phallic (sex) religion. The Phallic
religion seems to have been practiced in all parts of the world; evi-
dences and remains of that peculiar belief have been found in nearly
all quarters of the globe. True Phallic stones have been discovered
in abundance in all parts of North and South America; the western
parts of North America being especially prolific. At the time when
this was the prevailing religious belief, the priesthood wielded such
power over the people that it became a custom of the priests to bless
everything. The people were taught that the tilling of the soil—the
sowing of the seed, the harvesting and garnering of the grain—all ag-
ricultural operations—were only to be sanctified by the blessing of the
priest. Enterprises of all kinds, public and private, must receive the
attention of the priest in order to be approved by the divine spirit of
God. This divinity was supposed to manifest itself through the sexual
organs.

Monuments, exact images of the male organ, were erected in
public places. Numerous cunning devices were resorted to by priest
and politician in their religious and political teachings, all with an eye
single to perpetuating their hold upon the confiding people. Indeed,
the ignorance and faith of the people were so imposed upon that the
belief that a maiden must be blessed and fertilized by the priest before

she was fitted to meet the bridegroom in marriage relation became firmly established. Being fertilized by God, her progeny would, of course, be blessed, and as every bearing womb was thus dedicated to God so humanity would become blessed. Thus may be traced the origin of priestly vows of celibacy, of chastity, of silent meditation, of purity of mind, body and soul, imposed upon the candidate for priestly honors. The origin of the appellation "father" is made fearfully clear. It is a canon of the Roman Catholic Church that the Pope of Rome is a direct descendant of God through St. Peter. God being the father of the race and the Pope His earthly representative, the latter is called the "Holy Father." The priesthood of that church being His children logically they are entitled to the same appellation. The title "father," as applied to the priesthood, however, dates back to the period in this world's history when that portion of the earth now surrounding the north pole was the equator, the period preceding the world's change of polarity or axis.

This is written in no spirit of disrespect for the spiritual teachers of to-day. The writer believes them to be, as a class, honest, conscientious workers, who, like the rest of humanity, are looking at and contemplating the letter instead of the spirit. They, like their followers, are worshiping the symbol instead of the principle. It is a pure case of the blind leading the blind. The people and the priest think they have hold of the life, whereas really, they have only the symbol of the life. And while the symbol is grand, glorious—even sublime—and capable of much good, *it* is not to be compared in grandeur, sublimity and simplicity with the real truth itself.

The immaculate conception, lowly birth, ministry betrayal, crucifixion, all, are symbols of the laws of nature, and are applicable to each and every individual. In fact, the entire story of Christ is a history of the individual soul of mankind; sooner or later, every soul does for itself and humanity just what Christ did.

The works and life of Christ can be reduced to three points:

1. His recognition of God as the universal spirit permeating all things: the source of all life, light and substance.

2. He recognized himself as the son-child or part of that spirit, made in its image and likeness.

3. He recognized humanity collectively and individually as at one with himself, therefore at one with God, thus making God, the Universe, and man, *one*.

If this be true, how can there be any room for controversy, between good and evil?

Where is there any evil?

HUMANITY A UNIT

CHAPTER III.

"I AND MY FATHER ARE ONE"—"YE AND ME ARE BROTHERS"—"IF
I BE RAISED UP I DRAW ALL MEN UNTO ME"—THESE QUOTA-
TIONS FROM CHRIST ARE SIMPLE TRUTHS APPLICABLE TO
EVERY ONE—WE ARE ALL SAVIORS; WE ARE ALL JUDASES—
THEY ARE SYMBOLIC EXPRESSIONS OF LAWS OPERATING WITH-
IN EVERY PERSON—EVERY MAN A PROPHET; EVERY MAN THE
FULFILLMENT OF A PROPHECY—ALL ARE CRIMINALS; ALL ARE
EXECUTIONERS—PAST, PRESENT AND FUTURE BLENDED INTO
THE ETERNAL NOW—THE ASSASSINATION OF LINCOLN, GAR-
FIELD AND MCKINLEY LAID AT THE DOOR OF HUMANITY'S
THOUGHT—THE UNITED STATES A LIGHT-BEARER TO THE
WORLD.

HE SPOKE TO THEM IN PARABLES (SYMBOLS).

"I AND MY FATHER ARE ONE." "YE AND ME ARE BROTHERS." "IF
I BE LIFTED UP, I DRAW ALL MEN UNTO ME."

Every child is the embodiment of the hopes, aspirations, desires, fears, sins, failings, successes of its parents, i. e., every child is a

reflection of the mentality of the father and mother at time of conception. In its make up it is father, mother, plus itself; thus the two, male and female, uniting and giving their life or lives to the third, become one, and in this one they are perpetuated. Hence this *one* was, in the past, *two.*

Allowing twenty years for a generation and taking a retrospective view, we see that the two, (each having two parents) twenty years past were 4.

Those 4, 40 years previous, each having two parents, were 8.

Those 8, 60 years previous, each having two parents, were 16.

Those 16, 80 years previous, each having two parents were 32.

Those 32, 100 years previous, each having two parents, were 64.

Those 64, 120 years previous, each having two parents, were 128.

Those 128, 140 years previous, each having two parents, were 256.

Those 256, 160 years previous, each having two parents, were 512.

Those 512, 180 years previous, each having two parents, were 1024.

Those 1024, 200 years previous, each having two parents, were 2048.

Those 2048, 220 years previous, each having two parents, were 4096.

Those 4096, 240 years previous, each having two parents, were 8192.

Those 8192, 260 years previous, each having two parents, were 16,384.

Those 16,384, 280 years previous, each having two parents, were 32,768.

Those 32,768, 300 years previous, each having two parents, were 65,536.

Those 65,536, 320 years previous, each having two parents, were 131,072.

Those 131,072, 340 years previous, each having two parents, were 262,144.

Those 262,144, 360 years previous, each having two parents were 524,288.

Those 524,288, 380 years previous, each having two parents. were 1,048,576.

Those 1,048,576, 400 years previous, each having two parents. were 2,097,152.

If then, the individual of to-day is the embodiment of the virtues and sins of over 2,000,000 people in the short space of 400 years, is it any wonder that humanity struggles under its load?

God is always spoken of in the masculine gender. Who gave His only begotten Son that the world might be saved from death. And this law in nature which requires the father's life that the mother—earth—may be fertilized, simply means that the father becomes son and the son in his turn becomes father; thus every son can say with truth "I and my father are one."

Any new country, then, like the United States, which attracts to itself people from all parts of the world, naturally embodies in its make-up of citizenship a conglomerate condition of human evolution.

It was in 1492, or a little over 400 years ago, that America was discovered. Take the two million parentage of the child born to-day and scatter them over the face of the earth and behold, they would represent all conditions of humanity, such as statesmen, philosophers and philanthropists. They would also include the greatest scientists, the greatest criminals, the lowest degree of intelligence and the most abandoned indolence. By extending this calculation about 1000 years, or to the beginning of the Christian era, it will be seen that the child born to-day has within it the potentiality of all the people in the face of the earth. Thus the great Teacher, when he said, "And I, if I be lifted up from the earth will draw all men unto me," gave expression to a very simple truth. Every soul, then, is a redeemer of humanity, every soul is a Judas, and within every soul this continual strife for supremacy between good and evil is going on.

Who, then, can deny his brother, who can say aught against his fellowman, or accuse him of original sin?

We see great minds carrying out great enterprises; we admire generals for their gallantry; we worship the hero; we applaud the artist; we honor the statesman; but each one is the embodiment and expression of the hopes, desires, and ambitions of millions gone before. Perhaps they are the *fruitages* of millions of *failures* in their respective lines?

On the other hand we punish the criminal; we point the finger of scorn at the human failure whether it be a business or moral failure.

We despise the harlot, whether it be dressed in male or female garb; we shun the drunkard and execute the assasin; yet original sin is distributed equally among their parents and ours. They have an equal origin with us. How, then, can we say, "I am better than thou;" how can we, on this broad platform of universal fellowship and origin, deny our sonship of God and fraternal order of the brotherhood of man?

Reverse this process and look into the future. See how the individual of to-day with its hopes and fears, aspirations and desires, with its failings and shortcomings and sins and sorrows, breathes into its offspring, its self! Four hnndred years hence it will have distributed itself among two million people. Therefore, every individual is a culmination of some period. Every individual is the fruit of some hour and is the fulfillment of some prayer.

The Royal Arch Mason will see in this the law and the reason for the grand lesson of charity taught him when he himself imitates the great Teacher.

We are all saints—we are all sinners—therefore entitled to our reward when "right," and to forgiveness when "wrong." Did not Christ, true to His character as Mediator, ask forgiveness for his persecutors, even though there were included in their midst criminals of all kinds and degrees? As a collective whole, because of having put Christ to death they were murderers; yet he exclaimed with his dying breath: "Father, forgive them, for they know not what they do." The lesson here taught is one of stern, hard realities. It would teach us that any one of us, under the same conditions, under the same circumstances, might be guilty of the same offense or express the same virtue.

It would teach us to be more charitable to ourselves; to praise ourselves more, and to praise God less, realizing that our every act has its fruitage either in our own or some one's else life. It unmasks the hypocrite and reveals him in his frightful hideousness to his own eyes; by this law he is perforce buried in his own offal. Consequently none can say of the Lord, "He is just," or, "He is unjust." Each is the arbiter of his own destiny, yet all are interdependent. The concern of one is the concern of all.

Judas the betrayer, he who so loved money that he was willing to turn traitor, was as essential to the carrying out of God's plans as any of the prominent characters of his day. Without him the works of Christ would have been abortive. He betrayed himself, and he who will betray himself will also betray his family, betray his nation. Christ was true to *himself* though it cost him his life, yet the result was humanity's gain.

When he saw a martyr riding in an ox cart through the public streets, on the way to the guillotine, it was John Bunyan who said, "But for the grace of God there goes John Bunyan."

It is difficult to grant to the criminal the justice of his crime; nevertheless he is carrying out—putting into execution—the desires of his forefathers. He is quite as much the fruit of the tree of life as is the sculptor, the statesman, the general or the poet.

If humanity never desired the life of a fellow human being there would be no war, there would be no killing, there would be no taking of life, there would be no instruments of death nor of torture; but humanity thinks death, torture, and pain, toward his brother man. And at some place, at some time, that prayer is answered, and, of course only through human instrumentality.

Scan the classified advertisements in the daily press. Whole columns are filled with notices of rates, terms, secret conditions and other advantages offered by those who are in the "business" of taking the embryonic life for a consideration. Their calling prevents them from placing any other value upon human life than a monetary one.

The war general of the past, fighting with primitive weapons, wished—prayed, if you please—for a device which would enable him to kill whole battalions at one fell blow. He died wishing in vain, but has not his mediaeval prayer found fruitage in the invention of the machine gun and other implements of modern warfare?

The patient, persevering, silent working chemist in his laboratory seeking to discover some high explosive may be a kind, indulgent father, and a virtuous man; still he is the embodiment of the wish to take life. The architect of the modern "man-of-war," albeit a respected citizen, plans the destruction of nations; in his mind such thoughts are realities. He is a destroyer of life on the mental plane. The world calls him great and gives him credit for making something new—for creating something—yet to say that he is simply "a recorder of thought" may, after all, be nearer the truth. If the reader question this truth let him make a record, this minute, of his thoughts of the next minute.

"Those who intensify the force of cruelty in the place where they reside may be strengthening a murderer's hand to strike the deadly blow in a distant land."—W. J. Colville.

Ofttimes human desire finds sudden fruitage. To illustrate, a mother wishes to be rid of her unborn babe; she thinks murder, she prays its life may be taken that she may be relieved of the pain and sacrifice attendant upon birth; she desires its life be taken. She gives birth to the principle of murder, and ofttimes her child early develops life-taking propensities and becomes a natural criminal. It is unnecessary here to point out the many instances of sudden and unexpected fruitage of human desire, in this direction.

The so-called modern or New Thought that man is a creator, is gaining ground rapidly, finding many converts among the highest minds in the world. Men of greatest scientific attainment are recognizing and adopting the philosophy advanced by this new school of thought. While it would seem that man is a God in embryo, still, on the other hand, he is an instrument working out the principles and plans of his predecessor. However he, in turn, becomes a predecessor to coming generations; in this sense he is a creator. Thus man stands between the two great extremes. The eternal past and the eternal future are united in the everlasting present. Man stands in the "now." The vail between himself and the future is hermetically sealed, the book of the past indelibly written.

One of the prevailing hopes and beliefs of humanity is that when we pass into the next world, or after death, we are to meet our immediate relatives. If this be true, if every soul meet its parent soul, we will at once be reabsorbed into the all one. For if I meet *my* mother and father immediately after death, is it not also true that they met *their* father and mother immediately after death and every father and mother met *their* ancestry, and so on, ad infinitum?

If all our ancestry had been met at the river of death by their immediate ancestors then surely the eternal past is merged into the immediate present. We prove the truthfulness of this by the fact that we have but little interest or love for our ancestry beyond the grandparents. It is our *immediate* father and mother, brother or sister whom we expect to meet at the door of the sepulchre. If every son and daughter has been met by his own parents it is plain that all of the past is now rolled up to the present, and, using the living of to-day as media, stretches forth into the future. Thus does man stand eternally in the present; now is the only time he has. "All men have my blood and I have all men's," says Emerson.

Camille Flammarion wrote: "A human being dies every second upon the whole surface of the terrestrial globe—that is to say, about

86,400 persons die every day, 31,000,000 a year, or more than three hundred millions in a century. In ten centuries thirty thousand millions of corpses have been given to the earth; returned to atmospheric circulation in the form of water, gases, vapor, etc. The earth we inhabit is to-day formed in part of the myriad of brains which have thought, of the myriad of organisms which have lived. We walk over our ancestors as those who come after will walk over us.

"The brows of the thinkers; the eyes which have looked, smiled, wept; the lips which have sung of love; the arms of the worker; the muscles of the warrior; the blood of the vanquished; youth and age; the rich and the poor alike, all who have lived, all who have thought, lie in the same earth. It would be difficult at this day to take a single step upon this planet without walking over the remains of the dead. It would be difficult to eat and drink without re-absorbing that which has been eaten and drunk thousands upon thousands of times already; it would be difficult to breathe without incorporating the air already breathed by those now dead."

Who among us, then, cannot also say, "And I, if I be lifted up from the earth, will draw all men unto me."

By the operation of this law the sum total of all human endeavor and thought may find expression in one individual, be he poet, sculptor, martyr, assassin or Christ. The downtrodden and oppressed subjects of tyrannical rulers have planned in secret the destruction of their king. Their plans have miscarried at the time, but who will deny that their prayers (the desires of the heart) have found answer and fruitage in the brains and hand of a Booth, the aim of a Guiteau or a Czolgosz, and that the crowned heads were spared that a Lincoln, a Garfield and a McKinley might be substituted.

"He who would be greatest among you, let him be your servant," is a law. None of us would decline the honor of a Christ if we could escape the crucifixion?

Thus every human being is the culminating apex of some line of thought; the embodiment of some desire, some wish, some hope. Who among us, then, cannot also say: "And I, if I be lifted up from the earth, will draw all men unto me?"

Nations, like individuals, have their constituent and component parts, made up of still more minor parts until finally the nation resolves itself into the individual. The prevailing thought of the individual is a prophecy of the destiny of the nation.

The United States has been peopled by a race who wished to be free from despotic rule; who do not believe that one person's birth is more divine than another, and therefore that no one has a Divine right to rule autocratically; that in the sight of God all are born equal and of right ought to be free.

The United States is peopled by a race who have recognized the law of human equality. She has taken her place among the nations of earth as a peace maker. Her enforcement of the "Monroe doctrine" and her policy in dealing with the West Indian islands and the Philippines are living testimony to this fact. As a nation she is simply the fulfillment of the hopes, prayers and ambitions of the people of all nations for centuries of time.

Previous to the discovery of America and the establishment of this government it was impossible to teach the laws of nature on account of the strong hold the church had upon the people. As the life and prosperity of the church as well as its priesthood depended upon the *ignorance, fear* and *selfishness* of its votaries it was to the interest.

of the church to kill all desire in the minds of the people to know anything of the laws of God as expressed in the three worlds of Spirit, Soul and Matter, since to do so would be to take from the priest or preacher his power.

Until the United States was born there existed no nation which vouchsafed freedom of speech, of press and of person; it was absolutely necessary that the laws of God be taught in secret. It was necessary to impose the most sacred obligations upon the candidate for such teachings and to submit him to the most impressive ceremonies in order to make the deep impressions necessary to insure safe keeping of the knowledge to be imparted.

Real, all and absolute truth was never revealed in their secret lodges; only a substitute knowledge was given and that only in symbols, leaving the poor candidate to search for himself for the hidden treasure.

The world is not yet free; America is not yet fully prepared to carry the lighted torch of freedom to all the nations. The law is not yet fulfilled, but the day dawn is near.

The necessity for teaching Geometry in secret no longer exists.

The necessity for witholding the truth on the part of the church, as regards the true nature of God, no longer exists. Colleges and seminaries are too numerous to permit of further delay.

The seven seals of the Book of Revelation have been broken; the little book that was in the hand of the angel, and which was given to John to eat up is the ancient mystic test book of 52 pages known as the Deck of Playing Cards. It is the ancient Masonic Bible that reveals the laws of life. Until now it has been sealed up and entrusted to the custody of the vicious (?) ignorant (?) and wicked (?) people, those ancient brothers knowing that the people could always be trusted to preserve a plaything.

The infant "truth" (spirituality) has been discovered among the bullrushes by the side of the river of humanity, and it demands an equal chance to grow along with material science.

Masonry does not evangelize; its members must seek. In this respect it imitates Mother Nature who never reveals her charms to the indolent and unworthy but from those who seek in faith she withholds nothing. God solicits no one, but responds to every human cry.

Salvation seeks none, but is open to all. The angels of heaven do not go about with warrants to serve.

Masonry and the church, in imitation of heaven, elects no honorary members. God and salvation have no favorites. Each and every one must earn his bread, his corn, his wine.

The doors of immigration to the United States are open to all, yet seeking and soliciting none. Each is welcome; each finds a home and an opportunity to express freely his own self.

SUBJECT OF SYMBOLISM

CHAPTER IV.

NATURE ITSELF ONE VAST SYMBOL—MASONRY AND CATHOLICISM RICH FIELDS IN SYMBOLISM FOR THE MYSTIC STUDENT—SOUL, SPIRIT AND MATTER DEFINED—THE CHRISTIAN CROSS IN SYMBOLISM A PICTURE OF THE MALE ORGAN—THE CIRCLE AND SQUARE A PICTURE OF THE FEMALE ORGAN—HOW HUMANITY UNCONSCIOUSLY IS PERPETUATING THE OLD PHALLIC RELIGION —THE BIBLE ACCOUNT OF NOAH'S ARK AND THE TWO PILLARS OF MASONRY SHOWN TO BE A KINDERGARTEN STORY OF THE PERPETUATION OF THE ANIMAL SPECIES THROUGH THE BLENDING OF THE SEXES.

The subject of Symbolism is exceedingly interesting: It inspires the spirit of adventure and stimulates the desire for more knowledge of the unknown.

Nature itself is one vast symbol, for back of every object is the Spirit or Animating Principle. Therefore, the object is not the thing, but the *symbol* of the thing behind it. The object may perish; the principle lives on. Thus every man is a symbol, the embodiment of a principle. The principle does not die at the death of the body; it lives on and on. Nature presents her symbols to us and adds nothing by way of explanation. She is a great school in which each individual member divines her lesson from a different standpoint.

The student of Symbolism will find a rich field for investigation in the direction of Masonry by reading such books on the subject as may be found in the public book stores.

Catholicism is another equally rich field that invites the attention of the mystic student. The Bible is the monitor of both these schools of thought. Both receive their inspiration from the same source. The Bible is written from beginning to end in symbolic language.

After years of study in this fascinating subject, I find my utter incapacity to do it justice.

Let me, first of all, give credit to Mr. Olney H. Richmond for having started me on the pathway that leads to unfathomable mines of knowledge of mystical nature.

Mr. Richmond is one of the few great light bearers of the world, and in his "Mystic Test Book," published in 1893, will be found a vast amount of information that the student of mysteries cannot afford to be without. He it was who first proved to me that the deck of playing cards was the Sacred Book and was the absolute infallible key which would unlock the secrets of the universe.

Leaves fall and flowers decay but the life-giving force is born again the following season, presenting to the student the same symbol or form. For convenience of terms call this symbol "Matter" and the animating principle "Spirit."

Back of Matter then is Spirit, and back of Spirit is "Soul."

Spirit cannot be seen and comprehended from the standpoint of Matter, neither can the Soul Realm be comprehended from the standpoint of Spirit.

Soul is sexless.

Spirit and Matter have gender.

Soul penetrates and interprets all conditions of Spirit and Matter.

Soul is the neutral quality.

Soul is creative.

In the Soul realm there is no shadow.

In the Soul realm there is no symbol.

It is the firmament.

In the Soul realm there is but one language; there is no diversity of form; there is nothing hidden; there is no such thing as degree of goodness. Therefore nationality, race, color and distinction are unknown.

By Soul realm is not meant a place, but rather a condition possible for anyone to attain and be conscious of the attainment.

Many people have glimpses of this Soul realm, but on account of the fact that human language cannot express the condition, no one can describe it. To describe it by words, either written or spoken, would necessitate the use of symbols and the Soul realm cannot be described by symbol, as a symbol is not the real thing but the shadow.

A letter in any alphabet is a symbol of a universal law. A group of letters forming a word becomes the symbol of a larger law.

All rites, ceremonies, and forms are symbolical of universal laws (not practiced for the first and only time on this planet, but known on other worlds). (See explanation of Chart No. 2.)

Man is an expression of God and at the same time a symbol of what God is. Man worships God and at the same time God worships man, for in man God is glorified. As man sees himself reflected in his children so God sees in man himself portrayed.

In the Soul realm we come nearest to God and find there no diversity of tongues.

The Soul realm is in no special place; it is everywhere. It passes through worlds and suns and systems of worlds without disturbing their molecular construction. As the air passes freely between the forest trees so the realm of Soul passes freely through our bodies without disturbing the atomic construction. We are in it all the time; it is in us all the time. Each is unconscious of the other's presence. We are never away from it; it is never separated from us.

What is true of the Soul realm is also true of the Spirit world. Spirit, Soul and Matter, then, are eternally co-existent.

We say God is the source of all life, yet we cannot conceive of life without motion, and where motion is there must be something to move; if there is something to move, then the *materialist* must be correct when he declares "all is matter."

Matter cannot move without something to move it, and if the moving power be spirit, mind, or energy, then the other side is correct when they declare that *"all is Spirit," "all is mind," "all is gravity."* Without Spirit, matter is dead, dark, cold, and must, of course, be in a negative or receptive condition. Thus it being true that Spirit is life, light and heat, the former may be said to be the polar opposite to matter, but these two cannot unite of themselves. There must be a flux, or third element, which can partake of the nature and elements of both, and yet be neither one, in which Spirit and Matter can join. Or, to put it another way, Soul joins Spirit and Matter together.

Man functions on all three planes while in the body. (After the death of the body he functions on two planes and finally on only one.) These three planes, being eternally self-existent and co-existent, can best be symbolized by the triangle.

But there are many other "threes" for which the triangle might and does stand.

Christ said "Ye and me are brothers," "I and my father are one."

Then the triangle to the Christian might mean: The world of humanity as represented by one side of the triangle, Christ by the other side, and God by the third.

In the building of King Solomon's temple there were three prominent personages, two kings and a widow's son. These three might be represented by the triangle and mean much to the Masonic brother.

In electricity the triangle may be used to mean the positive, negative and neutral qualities of that subtle force. Thus, in the study of Symbolism, oftentimes the same symbol will stand for different laws conveying to different students entirely different meanings. For instance, the cross

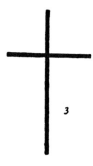

conveys to the Christian the idea of Christ being crucified. It means torture, and whenever the Christian sees the picture or image of a cross cut in marble or carved in wood, he naturally pictures in his mind the time when Christ was suspended on the cross; consequently he associates with the picture much pain and inhumanity of feeling.

To the astrologer the cross means far more than this: he adds to his knowledge of the Christian belief a knowledge of planetary laws; thus he gives to the cross a double interpretation.

To the mystic the cross is the picture of the male sex organs stripped of all embellishments.

Two straight lines crossed at right angles cannot possibly convey any unchaste thoughts to the beholder? Thus the reader will readily see the wisdom of those ancient brothers who preserved for us the wisdom of the ages in such innocent pictures as the cross, circle, triangle, and square; yet in these symbols is told the story of creation; how God the Father (Spirit) meets Earth (Matter), mother in sex relation.

Humanity unconsciously is preserving the sacred symbols and perpetuating the language in a thousand ways.

Look at the patterns in your carpets, window curtains, tapestry, furniture and all house decorations, and see how prominent is the cross, the circle, the triangle, the square. Behold in these the many references to the male and female organs, for, be it remembered, the square and circle is a picture (to the mystic) of the female organ.

In no place, however, does humanity perpetuate the union of Spirit and Matter so beautifully and innocently as in the building of houses of worship, for see, all churches are built square and surmounted with a tall spire which has a cross at the top. They are called "God's meeting-houses" or places of worship.

Now let us see how beautiful is the study of Symbolism. We speak of God as being masculine, "He," and to make the picture of the masculine principle without being sensual or calling forth criticism we have to make a picture of a cross thus

In the world of Matter there are four universal elements, viz: fire, earth, air and water. These elements, being equally distributed, can be represented by four straight and equal lines joined together thus,

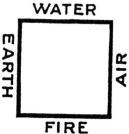

Matter is always being fertilized by Spirit, and is always referred to as "Mother Earth." She receives Him, the Spirit or God, and when these two ruling elements meet it is a meeting of the Gods.

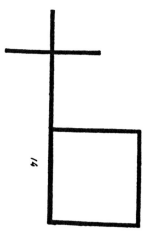

Join these two symbols together then—the square and cross—and we have a very good picture of the modern meeting-house.

Where Spirit and Matter meet creation is the result, or, if you please, salvation, for to create anew is to save from death. In the Bible story of the flood the same story is told in different languages, the same symbols being used, except in the case of the female symbol the circle is used instead of the square.

A covenant means an agreement between two or more, and when the male and female make a covenant or agree to perpetuate, they do so in the waters of gestation; hence the ark or arch of the covenant is represented in the Bible story as floating on the water.

The Crescent is made by "nesting" one-half of the circle within the other half thus

The reader can readily see that if these two halves were not "nested" it would be a true picture of the female organ.

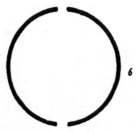

Add to this picture of the feminine principle the picture of the male principle and we have

Now let us add to these two a third, the "waters" of life and we have

or a boat with a sail up. God caused two of a kind of all his creatures to go into the ark (arch)

for the preservation of their species and thus to be saved from death; it is in the waters of gestation that all covenants for the perpetuation of life takes place. Thus the story of Noah and the ark is a kindergarten story of the all-preserving power of the God of nature working in that grand arch of the Heavens which reaches from horizon to horizon in which is all manner of life.

In Masonry the same story is told in another form. Here "two pillars" at the gateway are substituted for the male and female organs. The candidate's attention is called to these two pillars and Bible reference given, but the real truth regarding the law is never revealed in the lodge room. The candidate is left to dig for himself such meanings as his inspirations may bring. One of these pillars is a symbol of strength, power, majesty; the other beauty, harmony, symmetry; between these two the candidate enters the temple.

Masonry and Christianity are polar opposites, yet both teach the same laws and by the same means, viz: Symbols. The Christian is required to have faith only, while the Mason adds to his faith knowledge.

Question: What is a Mason?

Answer: A builder.

Q.: A builder of what?

A.: A temple.

Q.: To whom is the temple dedicated?

A.: To God.

Q.: What is the difference then between the Christian and the Mason?

A.: None whatever; both are seeking that freedom from limitations of matter imposed upon the incarnated soul; or, to express it in another way, the soul in its human embodiments is constantly striving to raise dead, inert matter to a consciousness of life eternal. The soul is the master builder; it alone being sexless can give to matter the germ of life necessary to raise "a dead thing" to life eternal.

The home of the soul has no limitations, but includes all suns and systems of suns seen and unseen.

It has no knowledge of time, as time is simply the measurement of moving bodies.

The Spirit is limited by the solar universe, and the orbit of Neptune marks the confines of Spirit power of this solar system.

The home of the body is the earth on which it is born.

Each sun and earth has its orbit; consequently each has its light side and shadow.

As worlds revolve about their parent suns one half is in shadow or asleep; thus there is always a grand arch in the heavens reaching from horizon to horizon. That arch in which the sun is may be called the circle of light, the opposite arch the circle of death and darkness. If these two great half circles be divided into six equal parts the result could be illustrated in some such manner as is represented in cut No. 1.

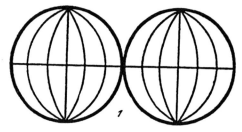

Of course this illustrates the twelve signs of the Zodiac.

Now if there be added to this picture or symbol the path of the sun, or lord, or master, of this great temple, we would have a picture like that in No. *2.

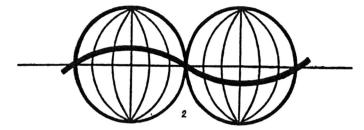

The curved line shows the path of the sun through the twelve signs of the Zodiac: its ascension and declination.

The sun being the Lord of the universe, continually moving from

*For a more complete explanation of this cut the reader is referred to the "Devil's Pulpit," by Sir Robert Taylor.

sign to sign, house to house, degree to degree, he is constantly converting to himself, as it were, the signs, houses and degrees as fast as he comes into them. He is always the same, yet on account of the change of position, relatively, being nearer to the earth at one time, at another farther away, these changes bring us a new Lord, who, however, is the same Lord with a different influence; consequently he is entitled to a new name. Thus every day in the year the Catholic celebrates in honor of some saint or new principle emanating from the same Lord.

PART IV.

MORE   PREPARATION   OF
THE   STUDENT   FOR   THE
GRAND LIGHT WHICH IS TO
BE REVEALED—MORE INTRO-
DUCTION.

THE TWENTY-TWO LET-
TERS OF THE HEBREW AL-
PHABET ARE, AT THIS TIME,
INTRODUCED TO THE READ-
ER FOR HIS CONSIDERATION.
THE CUTS ARE REPRODUC-
TIONS TAKEN FROM THE
"TAROT OF THE BOHEMIANS."
THE EXPLANATIONS, GIVEN
BY PAPUS, ARE IN SOLID
TYPE.

THE READER WILL GAIN
FROM A STUDY OF THESE
TWENTY-TWO LETTERS, OR
CARDS, A FOUNDATION FOR
THE LAW OF READING CHAR-
ACTER BY NAME—EACH LET-
TER IN A NAME REPRESENTS
A LAW, A NUMBER AND A
FORM.

SYMBOLISM.

CHAPTER V.

TAROT OF THE BOHEMIAN

THE JUGGLER.

FIRST LETTER—ALEPH.

The first letter of the Hebrew alphabet and the law it represents is well depicted by the "Juggler." From this hieroglyphic meaning are derived ideas of the unity of the principle which determines it, man or microcosm. The unity is the meaning of the primitive hieroglyphic. Attentive consideration of the first card of the Tarot will give us much light. If we take the first card of the Tarot and examine it attentively we will see that the form of the "Juggler" corresponds in all points with that of the first letter of the Hebrew alphabet. The top of the figure is occupied by the divine sign of universal life (OO) placed upon the head of the "Juggler." The bottom of the figure represents the earth ornamented with its productions (see The Vegetable Life). Lastly the center is occupied by man himself placed behind a table covered with divers objects. The right and the left of the figure are occupied by the hands of the "Juggler" one of them pointing toward the earth, the other raised toward heaven. The position of the hands represents the two principles, active and passive, of the great All, and it corresponds with the two columns *Jakin* and *Bohas* of the temple of Solomon and of Freemasonry. Man with one hand seeks for God in heaven; with the other he plunges below to call up the demon to himself, thus uniting the Divine and Diabolical in Humanity. In this way The Tarot shows us the role of the universal mediator accorded to man. The "Juggler" holds in the left hand the wand of the magi which he raises, and the four great symbols of he Tarot are placed before him, namely: the cup, the sword, the penticles, the scepter. The four great symbols are placed upon the table at random. Man must rule and arrange them. *God, Man* and the *Universe* are then the three meanings of the first card.

In our modern, or the common, deck of playing cards of fifty-two we have four Knaves or Jacks who correspond exactly hiero-glyphically with this "Juggler," for they picture forth the same law, namely, that of mediator. In the Christian religion, this law was em-bodied in Christ who said, "I and my Father are one, ye and me are brothers," thus declaring his connection as mediator between the Su-preme and Humanity. This same law is also pictured forth in the his-tory of Adam. The Biblical history of Adam and his work is here set forth in symbol, for be it remembered, Adam was told to "till the ground and to cause it to bring forth." The Lord caused all created things to pass in review before Adam. Adam gave each its name; thus was he in the position of the "Juggler," for the "Juggler" must be master of the things with which he juggles. They must obey him; they must be subservient to his slightest wish. Therefore, Adam being able to name all things, was master of all creation below him. He rep-resented the crowning effort of God in that Epoch. The human fac-ulty symbolized by the first card is that of the will or conscience. The physical body is represented by the earth upon which the "Jug-gler" stands. The realm of mind or conscience is represented by the divine sign of universal life (◯◯). Man, then, stands between these two extremes, so to speak, and every thought must be weighed by him before he acts, and every act is the result of deliberation which must be sanctioned by his conscience.   Thus man is eternally creating, building or destroying whithersoever he is tending, whether he makes for involution or evolution—both of which laws are indicated by the hands of the "Juggler," one of which points up and the other down.

THE HIGH PRIESTESS

SECOND LETTER—BETH.

God himself or God the Father reflects himself and gives birth to God the Man or God the Son, the negative relatively to his Creator. As we have seen, man is the divine receiver, therefore this card of The Tarot will express all the ideas of the first card received negatively. The first card represents a man standing. This on the contrary bears the figure of a woman seated. (This is the first idea of passivity.) The man endowed with all the attributes of power was placed within the midst of nature (Adam). The woman is adorned with all the attributes of authority and persuasion (Eve), and she is placed under the porch of Isis between two columns (idea of the sacred dwelling of the divine recipient). The two columns, like the arms of the "Juggler," express the positive and the negative. The woman wears a triple crown surmounted by the Lunar Crescent. She is enveloped in a transparent veil falling over her face. On her breast she bears the Solar Cross and upon her knees lies an open book. This is the picture of Isis, of Nature, whose veil must not be raised before the profane. The book indicates that the doctrines of Isis are hidden but that she divulges to the Magi the secrets of the true Kabbalah and of occult science.

It will be seen that associated with the High Priestess is also the tiled floor. The white and the black squares is another picture of the male and female elements in nature, the black square representing the feminine and the white the masculine. Every atom of matter of which the earth is formed is either male or female, and as we walk the surface of the earth we are constantly reminded of this universal law; and the great tyler of the universal lodge has prepared the lodge for our introduction and enlightenment. As the earth receives the light from the sun and as within the earth are the seeds of all creation, so she must be fertilized by the rays of the masculine sun. She (the earth) must receive his fire, his life. She must nurture the seed, she must bring it forth and bear it anew. As nature responds to the planetary motions so the High Priestess is crowned with a triple crown; this in turn is crowned by the moon. This is a beautiful way of telling in picture language of the three months of gestation. During the first three months of conception it is possible to separate the embryo from the mother; after the three months (or moon) to separate means death. It is at the third month (or moon) that the heart makes its first pulsation. Thus is life established or the connections made between the incarnating soul and mother earth—the physical body. The open book is a symbol of the fact that Mother Nature, by our deeds, writes our life, and it is in Mother Nature that we must look to find the secrets of life—the law governing our being. It will be observed also that in the hands are carried two keys, one of which is the key of inspiration, the other the key to deeds of nobleness and of those qualities which go to make up progress. It is the key that unlocks to us the secrets of our higher nature and spurs us on to a realization of a clear conscience which must follow a noble impulse. The other key opens to our vision a realization of despair, despondency and all of those conditions of the human mind that follow in the wake of a ravished conscience. Furthermore, these keys are symbols of authority; they are symbols of knowledge. One may have the knowledge but without opportunity his knowledge will not benefit him.

Woman is as much a ruler as her brother, man. Her strength as a ruler lies in her power to conceive. If she conceives for good she will unlock for humanity the secrets of Nature toward evolution. If she conceives for evil, then her offspring will sink to the lowest depths of degradation and prove the law of involution. It is the principle she conceives, and it is principle she will bring forth incarnate as flesh, blood and bone.

THE EMPRESS

THIRD LETTER—GIMEL.

The hieroglyphic meaning of this third letter is the throat; hence it signifies all that encloses—all that is hollow; a canal—an enclosure.

The throat is a spot where the words conceived in the brain are formed. It is a symbol of the material envelopment of spiritual forms, of organic generation under all its forms. Generation is the mystery by which the spirit unites itself to matter—by which the Divine becomes human. This symbol therefore signifies ideas of generation, of embodiment in all the worlds.

The human being becomes corporeal in the womb of woman. This woman is represented with wings in the center of a radiating sun. This represents the idea of spirituality—of the vivified principle of all beings. She holds an eagle in her right hand (symbol of the soul of life). In the left hand, she bears a scepter. The scepter is in the left hand to indicate the passive influence which nature or the woman exercises in the generation of beings. She is crowned with nine stars, while the moon is placed under her feet. The stars refer to the nine months of gestation. The moon under the feet indicates that the waters of gestation (sometimes referred to as the river of life,) are under full or absolute control. The eagle astrologically belongs in the sign scorpio (sex organs). Therefore it will be seen that the nature of the card is constantly referring to that meaning.

THE EMPEROR

FOURTH LETTER—DALETH.

The meaning of the fourth letter (Daleth) is the womb. It suggests the idea of an object giving plentiful nourishment and a source of growth. It denotes abundance springing from division. It is the sign of active creation. This symbol, a man sitting in profile, holds in his right hand a scepter (symbol of generation). The man is bearded and wears a helmet. He is seated upon a cubic stone which bears the figure of an eagle. The man's legs are crossed. Divest the body of all flesh, the skeleton would describe a triangle surmounted by a cross, (**X**) "domination of the spirit over matter."

The helmet worn is a symbol of authority. The long full beard shows age, judgment, maturity. Carried in the left hand is a sphere surmounted by a cross. This is the symbol of Venus, the Goddess of

Love. The cube upon which the man is seated is a symbol of the four elements in nature, fire, earth, air, water.

The entire garb of the man is that of protection; therefore the predominating idea expressed by the symbol is that of protection— the natural result of wisdom gained by experience.

THE POPE

FIFTH LETTER—HE.

The hieroglyphic meaning of this letter (He) is aspiration, breath. It is by aspiration that life is incessantly maintained and created. It is also the mediating principle which attaches the material body to the divine spirit in the same way that man unites God and nature. He is seated between the two columns of the sanctuary. He leans upon a triple cross and makes the sign of esoterism with his right hand. The triple cross represents the penetration of the creative power throughout the divine, the intellectual and physical worlds, which causes all the manifestations of universal life to appear. The two columns symbolize the law on the one hand and the liberty to obey or disobey on the other. He wears a tiara. Two grown men kneel at his feet. One is clothed in red, the other in black.

THE LOVERS

SIXTH LETTER—VAU.

The hieroglyphic sign for the sixth letter (Vau) is the eye. It is the eye that establishes the link between the external world and ourselves. By it light and form are revealed to us. The dominant idea expressed by this letter, therefore, is that of a connection, of a link between antagonists. It also represents reunion with all its consequences.

A youth, beardless and without a hat, is standing motionless in the angle where two roads meet. His arms form a diagonal cross upon his breast. Two women, one on his right, the other on his left, each with one hand upon his shoulder, point to the two roads. The woman upon the right has a circle of gold upon her head. The one upon the left is disheveled and crowned with vine leaves. The spirit of justice floats above this group in a radiant halo. He bends his bow and aims the arrow of punishment.

To explain the laws symbolized in this letter fully, would require a small volume. Briefly told, however, it pictures the constant struggle going on within the breast of every human being. Man does not know how to direct the magnetic currents of the Astral. He is, therefore, plunged in the antagonism of the different ideas, which he cannot master. The two columns of the temple of Isis expressing necessity and liberty are here personified by the two women who represent vice and virtue. The future of the young man depends upon the road which he chooses. The spirit of justice personified by the blindfold Cupid is a profound symbol indicating that if man chooses the path of virtue he will not be left unaided; but that providence will ally itself to his will and assist him to overcome vice. It also reminds us of the law that however low we may sink in the quagmires of degradation and crime, the angel of peace and virtue is still with us ready to stretch forth a helping hand. This is a symbol of the conscience in man— of the eternal struggle going on. Every thought is weighed by us before being acted upon and, whichever way we decide just reward awaits us. Punishment meted out to the criminal is his reward. Hours enjoyed by the exercise of a clear conscience is also a reward. This card symbolizes the fact that wherever man is, whatever his condition, he cannot escape the all-seeing Eye.

THE CHARIOT

SEVENTH LETTER—ZAIN.

The conqueror crowned with a coronet, upon which rise three shining pentagrams of gold, advances in a cubical chariot surmounted by an azure star-decked canopy supported by four columns. Two sphinxes, one white, one black, are harnessed to the chariot. The four columns represent the four elements in nature, fire, earth, air, water. The conqueror who occupies the center of the four elements is the man, who has vanquished and directed the elementary forces. This victory is confirmed by the cubical form of the chariot. The two sphinxes correspond to the two principles, acitve and passive. It shows the influence of the creation, in the preservation of the divine in the human, man performing the function of God the creator.

JUSTICE

EIGHTH LETTER—HETH.

Hieroglyphically this letter expresses a field. From it springs the idea of anything that requires labor, trouble and effort. Continued effort results in the establishment of an equilibrium between the destruction of the works of man accomplished by Nature when left to herself, and the preservation of this work, hence the idea balancing power, and consequently of justice attributed to this letter. The ideas expressed by this symbol are those of equilibrium in all its forms. The woman seen full face and wearing an iron coronet is seated upon a throne. She is placed between the two columns of the temple. She holds a sword pointed upwards in her right hand and a balance in her left.

Within the crown is the symbol of the sun ($\odot$). The woman crowned, or, rather, wearing in her crown a jewel of this nature shows eternal justice meted out to humanity by the universal soul. The same law is also pictured forth in the pair of balances held in the left hand.

THE HERMET

NINTH LETTER—TETH.

Hieroglyphically the ninth letter represents the roof and suggests the idea of a place of safety—protection derived from wisdom. An old man walking, supported by a stick. He carries before him a lighted lamp half hidden by the great mantle which envelops him, and a serpent precedes him. Experience won in the labor of life has rendered him a prudent old man, and prudence united to wisdom, (symbolized by the serpent), will safely lead him to the higher level which he is anxious to attain. The arrow shot by the genius in the sixth letter has become his support and an effulgent aureole which surrounded the genius is now imprisoned in the lamp which guides the initiate. This is the result of his prolonged efforts.

THE WHEEL OF FORTUNE

TENTH LETTER—YOD.

The Wheel of Fortune is suspended upon its axis, to the right the Genius of Good ascending, to the left the Genius of Evil descending. The sphinx is balanced upon the center of the wheel holding a sword in its lion claws.

The descending Genius carries in its hand a three pronged scepter, symbol of Neptune, god of water. The soul of man is baptized in the waters of gestation at conception and must control that element or perish in the attempt. Two serpents are seen at the base of the post rising from two boats or canoes which float upon a watery surface. This is again a symbol of gestation, and is another way of telling the story of Noah's Ark for, be it remembered, in Noah's Ark were gathered together two of a kind, male and female, of all living creatures; so here the two serpents representing male and female life floating upon the surface of the waters of life. The whole picture is crowned with the sphinx which embodies within itself the four Genii of the zodiac, namely, the Eagle, the Lion, the Man and the Bull, thus bringing into one comprehensive glance the entire animal world, also the four elements fire, earth, air, water.

STRENGTH

ELEVENTH LETTER—KAPH.

Two main ideas are expressed by this arcanum, first the idea of strength, second the idea of vitality. (A young girl calmly closing the mouth of a lion without any visible effort.) This young girl wears the vital sign upon her head.

This eleventh letter corresponds with the Christ principle as perceived in the Christian religion. This is a new way of picturing forth the *strength* of *law* and *soul* forces accumulated through a life of prayer. Whenever the Nazarene was troubled he retired into privacy and prayed; this always brought to him the strength necessary to undergo any ordeal. It is woman's refuge when in trouble to pray. It is also her first thought when all other supports are taken away. She finds comfort in prayer. It also removes fear. With fear entirely eradicated from our natures we can, like Daniel, face the elemental conditions represented in the picture by the lion. Thus the pure in heart shall not only see God but walk with Him and fear no evil.

"THE HANGED MAN"

TWELFTH LETTER—LAMED.

Hieroglyphically this letter designates the arm, therefore it is connected with anything that stretches, that raises, that enfolds—like the arm—and has become the sign of expansive movement. It is applied to all ideas of extension, of occupation, of possession. As a last sign, it is the image of power derived from elevation. Divine expansion in humanity is produced by the prophet's revelation, and this inspires the idea of the revealed law. But the revelation of the law involves punishment for him who violates it, or elevation for him who understands it; and here we find the ideas of punishment, of violent death, voluntary or involuntary.

The man's hands are tied behind his back and the fold of his arms forms the base of a reversed triangle, of which his head forms the point. His eyes are open and his fair hair floats upon the wind. His right leg crosses his left and so forms a cross. Like the sun placed in the midst of the signs of the zodiac our young hero is again suspended betwen two decisions from which will spring no longer his physical future (as in the sixth letter), but his spiritual future, for be it remembered, this is the same young man to whom we were first introduced in the first letter as the "Juggler"; again in the sixth lettter, where he stands between two contending forces personified by the two women; here he is again presented for our consideration, but this time suspended between two trees of life which have six branches. The hanged man serves as an example to the presumptuous, and his position indicates discipline, the absolute submission which the human owes to the divine. Considered alchemically, the hanged man shows the sign of personality (☿), the Hermetic Grade of the Rosy Cross (Eighteenth Degree of the Freemasonry of Scotland). One of the signs of recognition consists of crossing the legs like the legs of the hanged man. It is needless to say that the origin and meaning of this sign is quite unknown to the Freemasons.

DEATH

THIRTEENTH LETTER—MEM.

The hieroglyphic of this letter is a woman, the companion of men. It therefore gives rise to ideas of fertility and formation. It is preeminently the maternal, a female—the local and plastic sign—the image of external and passive action. Creation necessitates equal destruction in a contrary sense; therefore this letter designates all the regeneration that has sprung from previous destruction. All transformation, and consequently death, is regarded as a passage from one world to another. The ideas expressed by the skeleton mower are those of destruction preceding and following regeneration. The skeleton mows down heads in a field from which spring hands and feet on all sides as the scythe pursues its work.

A natural inquiry would arise in the reader's mind as to why this great symbol of death should be associated with woman. In all studies of occult science the female is always represented as the receiver of light, consequently, compared with light, she is dark. Therefore in the tiled floor, the dark squares are feminine, the light ones masculine. Our earth receives light from the sun; it is always spoken of in the feminine gender—she. The earth bosom is plowed and harrowed; she receives the seeds of the husbandman, and it is she who must bring forth her conceptions.

TEMPERANCE

FOURTEENTH LETTER—NUN.

The hieroglyphic of the fourteenth letter is the offspring of the female, a son, a fruit of any kind—all things produced. This letter has therefore become the image of the being produced of reflected, the sign of individual and corporeal existence. It expresses the production of any combination, the result of the action of the ascending or creating forces or of the descending or destructive forces figured by the star of Solomon. The Genius of the sun pours the fluid of life from a golden vessel into a silver one; this essence passes from one vase to the other without one drop being spilled.

The Genius of the sun is referred to by the sign of the sun placed on the forehead of the female figure.

THE DEVIL

FIFTEENTH LETTER—SAMECH.

In every cosmogony the Devil represents the mysterious astral forces, the origin of which is revealed to us by the extending of the law back of this fifteenth letter. A little attentive consideration of the picture will show us that it contains several of the details which we have already seen in other figures of The Tarot, but under a different aspect. If we place the "Juggler" by the side of the Devil we shall see that the arms of the two personages are using the *same* gesture but in an *inverce* sense. The "Juggler" opens his right hand toward the *universe*, his left toward *God*. On the other hand the Devil raises his right hand into the *air*, whilst his left points to the *earth*. Instead of the magic initiating wand of "The Juggler" the demon holds the ~~universe, his left toward God. On the other hand the Devil raises~~ balanced by him, are two personages reproducing the same symbolism that we find in the two women of the lover and in the two supports of the gibbet of "the Hanged Man." The universal vivifying forces represented by the third letter have here become the universal destroying force. The angel's wings have changed into the hideous pinions of the God of Evil. The Devil has materialized upon his head the universal fluid which surrounded the head of the "Juggler." This is indicated by the two six-pointed horns which adorn him. He stands upon a cube to indicate the domination of matter over spirit.

He wears an apron; upon it is painted the sign of Mercury which in turn is composed of a circle, half circle, and cross or sun, moon, and earth.

FIRE OF HEAVEN

SIXTEENTH LETTER—AYIN.

The nature of this letter is the sign of material sense again degenerated. It expresses all that is crooked, all that is perverse and bad. It contains an allusion to a material building. It signifies the invisible or spiritual world.

This is a beautiful picture setting forth the weakness of man when he isolates himself from God by his egotistic thinking. There are many sects and individuals claiming divine power for themselves, heralding perpetual life, claiming immortality for themselves, and still they are able in many instances to fool or deceive many. There comes a time when they, too, must obey the eternal laws of God and their building, which they supposed was constructed of stone and mortar and which they thought was proof against all destructive forces, yields to the lightning floods of those superior laws of which they were ignorant and which destroys them as readily as the minor law forces destroy less pretentious persons. So when we hear individuals laying claim to eternal life in the body we will, no doubt, recall the lightning struck tower.

THE STARS

SEVENTEENTH LETTER—PHE.

The seventeenth letter signifies the word *negation* in nature with all its consequences. Two ideas prominently set forth the first, by the *expansion* of astral fluids; second, by their eternal *renewal*—the nude female figure pouring the fluids of universal life from two cups. The Genius of the Sun represented in the fourteenth letter has now descended to earth under the form of this young girl, the image of eternal youth. The fluids which she formerly poured from one vase to another she now throws upon the ground. She is crowned with seven stars and in the midst of them shines a very large and brilliant one. By her a butterfly rests upon a flower. This is the symbol of immortality. The soul will survive the body which is only a place of trial. The courage to bear this trial will come from above (the stars). This letter pictures forth that law which exactly balances the evil effects of the preceding one; from it we derive the following signification: First, opposition to destruction (no destruction is final: everything is eternal and immortal in God). Second, the fall is not irreparable. This is whispered to us by the intuition ye name Hope. Third, the visible universe contains the source of its divinization in itself. This is the force which dispenses the essence of life, which gives the means of perpetually renewing its creations after destruction.

THE MOON

EIGHTEENTH LETTER—TZADDI.

A meadow feebly lighted by the moon. The light, the symbol of the soul, no longer reaches us directly. The material world is only lighted by reflection. The meadow is bounded by a tower on each side. The *material* world is the last point which the spirit can reach; it can descend no lower. This is shown by the boundary of the field. The drops of blood represent the descent of the spirit into matter. In the center of the field a dog and a wolf are baying the moon. A crawfish is climbing out of the water between the two animals. The entering of the spirit into matter is so great a fall that everything conspires to augment it: servile spirits (the dog), savage souls (the wolf), and crawling creatures (the crawfish), are all present watching the fall of the soul and hoping to aid in its destruction.

THE SUN

NINETEENTH LETTER—ZOPH.

Two naked children are shut into a walled enclosure. The sun sends down his rays upon them and drops of gold escape from him and fall upon the ground. The spirit resumes its ascendancy. It is no longer a reflected light as in the preceding arcanum, but a direct creative light of the God of our universe which floods it with his rays. The walls indicate that we are still in the visible or material world. The two children symbolize the two creative fluids, positive and negative, of the new creature. This letter symbolizes the awakening of the spirit, transition from the material world to the divine world after accomplishing the function of God. It also symbolizes the renewal of the body by motion. The material world commences its ascension toward God or evolution.

JUDGMENT

TWENTIETH LETTER—RESH.

An angel with fiery wings surrounded by a radiant halo sounds the trumpet of the last judgment. The instrument is decorated with a cross. A tomb opens in the earth, and a man, woman and child issue from it. Their hands are joined in the sign of adoration. How can the reawakening of nature under the influence of the word be better expressed? We must admire the way in which the symbol answers to the corresponding Hebrew hieroglyphic. This letter signifies: first, the return to the divine world, the spirit finally regains possession of itself; second, life renews itself by its own motion; third, the material world progresses one degree in its ascension toward God.

THE FOOL

TWENTY-FIRST LETTER—SHIN.

'A careless looking man, wearing a fool's cap and torn clothes, with a bundle upon his back, goes calmly upon his way paying no attention to a dog which bites his leg. He does not look where he is going, so walks toward a precipice where a crocodile is waiting to devour him. This is an image of the state to which unresisted passion will reduce a man. This is a symbol of the flesh and its gratification. The following verse from Eliphas Levy well explains this symbol:

"Sorrow lessens in work, not fulfilling a task,
Woe to the sluggard who sleeps on his way;
Like the dog at his heels pain clings to him fast
If he leave for to-morrow the work of to-day."

This is a picture of a wise fool. It is a wise man who knows the law, but he is a fool who does not do what he knows is right.

To a greater or less extent are not we all wise fools?

THE WORLD

TWENTY-SECOND LETTER—TAU.

The world and nude female figure holding the wand in her hand is placed in the center of an ellipsis, her legs crossed like those of the "Hanged Man." At the four angles of the card or picture we find the four animals of the apocalypse and the four forms of the sphinx; the man, the lion, the bull, and the eagle. This symbol represents macrocosm and microcosm, that is to say, God and creation, or the law of the absolute. The four figures placed at the four corners represent the four letters of the sacred name, or the four great symbols of the Tarot, namely, the scepter, the cup, the sword and the penticle, between the sacred word that signifies God. In the center of the figure is a circle, or ellipsis, representing nature and her regular and fatal course. From this comes the name of Rota, wheel, given to it by Guillaume Postel. Lastly, the center of the figure represents humanity. This letter, therefore, contains in itself a recapitulation of all previous ones.

PART V.

IN OUR SEARCH FOR *DI-VINE TRUTH* WE HAVE NOW ARRIVED AT THAT PART OF OUR JOURNEY WHERE THE GREAT VEIL MAY BE PULLED ASIDE AND STARTLING TRUTHS RE-GARDING ONE OF THE MOST COMMON BOOKS OF SYMBOLS IS MADE KNOWN TO THE READER. ALL PRE-CEDING PAGES HAVE BEEN DEVOTED TO A PREPARA-TION OF THE MIND FOR WHAT IS NOW TO FOLLOW, AND WITH FEELINGS OF REVERENCE AND LOVE THE AUTHOR ENTERS UPON AN INTERPRETATION OF THE DECK OF CARDS.

PART V.

CHAPTER VI.

THE DIVINE LANGUAGE OF THE PACK OF PLAYING CARDS—AS A
RECORD OF GOD'S SACRED AND INSPIRED WORD ITS AUTHEN-
TICITY IS SECOND TO NONE OTHER, BEING WRITTEN IN A LAN-
GUAGE UNIVERSAL, DEALING WITH THE LAWS OF SOUL, SPIRIT
AND BODY—THE FOUR SUITS AS EMBLEMS REFER TO THE FOUR
ELEMENTS IN NATURE: FIRE, EARTH, AIR AND WATER—THE
DIAMOND THE CROSS OF CHRIST; THE SPADE, AN ACORN; THE
HEART, A FLAME OF FIRE; THE CLUB, A CLOVER LEAF—THE
FOUR KINGS SYMBOLS OF LIFE AND DEATH.

The extended consideration vouchsafed the Tarot of the
Bohemians has been given with a view of introducing to the mind of
the reader and preparing him for consideration of that book which is
so well known throughout the world as "the deck of playing cards."
Sometimes it is called "the devil's prayer book," again, "the devil's picture book," "the book of 52," and many other appellations calculated
to convey to the mind anything but that of holiness. It is unnecessary at this time to produce evidence of antiquity for this little book.
It is equally unnecessary to produce evidence of its infallibility. But
to the student of nature and of symbolism who will study this book
with an unprejudiced mind it is a revelation of those laws governing
spirit, soul and body. It is referred to in the Bible in several places
but perhaps the most prominent is in the tenth chapter of Revelations,
and especially the ninth verse, which reads, "And I went unto the an-

gel, and said unto him, Give me the little book; and he said unto me,
Take it, and eat it up; and it shall make thy belly bitter, but it shall be
in thy mouth sweet as honey;" also the eleventh verse, "And he said
unto me, Thou must prophesy again before many peoples, and nations,
and tongues, and kings."

I do not wish to shock the sensibilities of my Masonic brethren,
nor cause my Christian brother to throw up his hands in holy horror,
but if to tell the truth regarding our deck of playing cards I should
reveal the "lost word" and open the sepulchre of the living Christ I
wash my hands of any responsibility. My sole desire is to throw more
light on this subject which has for ages been buried in the debris of
the temple of humanity.

That anything good can come from a deck of playing cards most
people will question; but I shall not speak of the book as cards but
rather by a more endearing term, the "little book;" and let me say to
the inquiring reader that a close study of the "little book" will furnish
not only a key to his own soul but will reveal to him Nature, for it is
truly a key to that heavenly home the whole world is seeking. It is
the only book written in a universal language; the only one with which
prophecies can be made. Every town, village, and community has its
prophet who uses this "little book" as a means of divination. It is
the only book a whole world is rolling under its tongue and finds
"sweet as honey," but let the world once digest its contents and become acquainted with the laws it reveals and—indeed, it will then be
bitter. The sweetness referred to is the pleasure derived from the
unholy use made of this sacred book.

In order to understand the "little book" let us consider it from
Nature's standpoint. We will find it is divided into two parts repre-

sented by the two colors which correspond with the spiritual and physical body spoken of in the Bible. They also refer to the two pillars at the entrance of the Masonic temple—male and female—called Strength and Beauty.

There are three court cards in each suit; these represent the three universal ruling principles in nature, positive, negative and neutral. Every atom and every world has its two poles and equator. These three universal ruling forces are represented by the King, Queen and Knave. The King and Queen symbolize the positive and negative qualities, the knave represents the neutral.

There are four suits corresponding with the four elemental forces in nature, viz: fire, earth, air, and water, but these four reduce themselves to one, and that one is fire.

HEART QUARTER.

Fire implies motion, motion vibration, and vibration carried to the extreme is light. Hence, as all things move whether in individual or in mass, fire becomes the symbol of universal life.

Nothing can have life except the life come from God, therefore the Heart, called the emblem of love, is really a flame of fire. In other words it is a picture of a lighted candle and has reference to that source of all life, God; hence, it symbolizes childhood, purity innocence and the first quarter of life from birth to twelve years of age at which time the man comes to puberty.

CLUB QUARTER.

From twelve to thirty man gathers wisdom and knowledge.

All wisdom comes from above, so the clover leaf is the most fitting symbol to represent the summertime of life, it being first to come in the spring and last to go in fall, and is universally found the world over. It is selected to symbolize universal knowledge. The leaf, perhaps, corresponds to the lungs of man; therefore the Club, or clover leaf, stands for air, also wisdom.

DIAMOND QUARTER.

The Diamond is a symbol of worldly wealth and power. The most precious thing on earth is a diamond. He who has diamonds has power among men. Man bends all his energy toward getting wealth, and from the age of thirty to eighty-four may be considered the fall or autumn of life, therefore the diamond corresponds to this period of life. There is, however, a deeper and more esoteric meaning to this beautiful symbol; it is simply a six sided cube and when opened out becomes the cross of Christ.

The cube has, in all ages, been held sacred. All altars were in the form of a cube or double cube.

The ancients esteemed the double cube as "holy" but the perfect or single cube as "most holy."

In the accompanying cut may be seen the six points of a double triangle, which interlaced would produce the six pointed star and in the center of the cut is the seventh *point*. Thus the Diamond, emblem of matter and cross of Christ, becomes the Masonic altar with the working tools engraved upon it. (Square and Compass.)

To make this cross proceed as follows: first, make the cube thus,

Fig. 1.

now raise the top side of the cube as though it were the top of a box

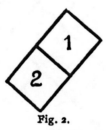

Fig. 2.

and you have fig 2. Now lower the bottom side of this cube or box and you have fig. 3; on the opposite side of face 1 is face 4,

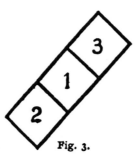

Fig. 3.

drop this down below face 3 and you have fig. 4. There are still
two other sides or faces to this cube; these opened out give us the ob-

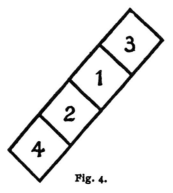

Fig. 4.

lique cross, fig. 5. This is the cross of matter so difficult to carry
and which Christ himself yielded up in pain and sorrow, for when the

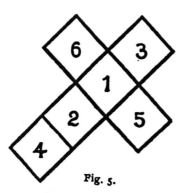

Fig. 5.

human soul, (a ray of light), seeks embodiment in matter, the matter being subject to the law of crystallization, this cube or diamond is

simply a picture of the cross or salt crystal into which the soul is immersed.

We all desire to be sons of God but the desires of the flesh and lusts of the body so encase the souls of men in utter darkness that the Diamond card very nicely symbolizes the Biblical expression, "Light shineth in the darkness and the darkness comprehendeth it not."

SPADE QUARTER.

After we pass the eighty-fourth year of earthly experience we enter into the fourth and last quarter of life. This transition is ofttimes marked by very pronounced physical changes, such as second sight, new hair, new teeth; sometimes a general rebuilding of the body. This age is often called second childhood. It is here we enter the last quarter of life, called the quarter of death. The implement used for digging the grave and to fill in the earth after the body has been deposited is called a spade and it becomes the symbol of death. In olden times there were no round-pointed shovels, such as we have in this day, hence this picture must have reference to something in nature; when we search nature we find the Spade bears a very strong resemblance to the acorn.

Here again we see how the masters of old have hidden the golden word of truth from the vandals and ruffians, for the Spade is not a spade but rather the picture of an acorn.

and to know what an acorn symbolizes in this connection we have but to study the history of an acorn. The acorn dies (falls) from the parent tree, is buried and rots in order that the germ may grow and come forth another tree. We find it has an outer shell, an inner meat, or kernel, and then the chit, or germ. The outer shell breaks, disintegrates, decays. The inner kernel or meat supports the germ for a short time and it, too, ceases existence. So must the individual man die from the parent tree of humanity and lay his mortal body away in the grave in order that the spirit and soul may be set free to return again to the bosom of the universal one.

Thus the acorn becomes a symbol of death, burial and resurrection, while the Spade speaks only of death and labor. If the "little book" has such wonderful truths to tell in so short a perusal, we may expect wonderful riches to be opened up to our gaze as we proceed with our investigation.

We will now consider the four Kings and see what nature has to tell us through them. Each wears long hair, full beards and the general facial expression shows strength, maturity, judgment. Each has associated with him instruments of death, as swords and battle-axes. There is a dual meaning to everything in connection with the cards, and these implements of warfare speak to us in a beautiful dual language. In the first place, however, the Kings represent the male principle in nature. Man rules by right of strength and knows no law by which he can become master except the law of extermination. Every obstacle in his pathway must be removed, forever exterminated. Thus the instruments of death symbolize man's ability to subdue. They also symbolize man's ability to take life and really picture the first stages of human development, where brother is arrayed against brother "even unto death." The history of the world up to the present time is one of the sword and battle-ax, for man has only recognized the law of physical might. On the spiritual or higher plane, these symbols tell of the higher law which says that the male, or man, in order to live must take his own life, not by the cowardly act of suicide but by the holy and divine law of marriage, for the male must always yield up his life's substance in order that the female may be fertilized; in doing so he voluntarily takes his own life. God is always spoken of in the masculine gender. He gave His only begotten Son that the world might be saved from death. This law in nature, that requires the father's life in order that the mother may be fertilized, simply means that the father becomes the son and the son becomes the father. Thus, every son can say with truth, "I and my father are one." So, too, every human soul has the same source and each can, with equal truth, say, "Ye and me are brothers." In order that the race may be perpetuated each man is endowed with generative powers, which power is his fire or life; and in order to perpetuate his kind, he is required to give this life to the world of matter or mother. Hence God as man is forever giving his life; therefore he says, speaking of life as symbolized by the battle-ax and sword, "I give and I take it away."

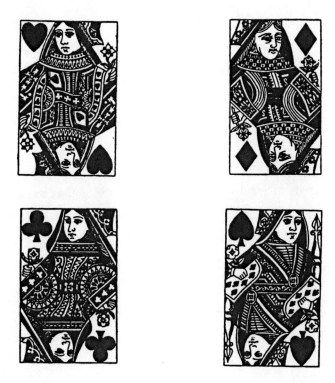

CHAPTER VII.

WOMAN A RULER AS WELL AS MAN—HER POWER TO RULE BEING
THE LAW OF CONCEPTION—THE FOUR JACKS SYMBOLS OF THE
NEUTER ELEMENT IN MATTER—ALSO SYMBOLS OF THE SOUL,
CONSCIENCE AND CHRIST PRINCIPLE—THE ATTITUDE OF THE
COURT CARDS SHOW A DESIRE FOR THE PRINCIPLE SYMBOLIZED
BY THE SUIT.

We will now consider the four Queens. We notice first the
entire absence of any implement or suggestion of death. Each shows

maturity and judgment. Each wears a crown, symbol of authority, showing that woman is as much a ruler as her brother and as much entitled to the throne as he. Their implements of authority are best symbolized by the flower carried in the hand of each. This is a beautiful symbol of life, of inspiration, of desire, of prayer, of hope. It is a symbol of the female principle in nature: it is in the springtime, when Mother Nature is in bloom, that the husbandmen go forth sowing the seeds of fertilization. It is in the flower that conception takes place: woman conceives, and that which is conceived must be brought forth. Hence, woman rules the world as much as man but her strength and ruling power lies in her conceptions, and that which she will conceive will be like her prayer, her hope, her ambition, her desire. All of which is symbolized by the open flower held in the hand.

All countries honor their heroes. The world has paid tribute to her great men—monuments of various kinds, costing immense fortunes, have been erected to men of genius in honor of their deeds of valor. But behind each man, behind each hero, behind each genius, there stands the mother who sees in her son the fulfillment of her hopes, her prayers. Man being the embodiment of principles, and as no great principle ever was or ever will be born until it is first conceived, the four Queens symbolize divine or peaceful conception.

The female receives the *fires of life* from the male but the *principle* is of her own conception. Inspiration can be and is exercised by both man and woman, hence, the principles symbolized by the Kings and Queens belong to both male and female throughout the universe, and it is just as natural for woman to conceive death through her thoughts as life. Hence she is equally capable of bringing forth either a murderer or a savior.

Before proceeding to the consideration of the Knaves let me call attention to the three forces in nature which are universal and inseparable. I refer to the planet upon which we life. It has a north pole, a south pole and an equator, the poles meeting at the equator or neutral point. The neutral is dependent upon the other two for its existence. The poles in turn meet at the neutral point, hence, the three are one and the one is three. What can be said of polarity as applied to the earth can also be said of the atom, for each atom has its positive, negative and neutral qualities.

A close examination of the four knaves reveals to us youthful faces. They have the court dress and crown, symbolizing the ruling principle—symbolizing to us that the neutral principle is just as constant, just as universal as the positive or negative and yet the former is never a *fixed principle*. It is ever changing, as the positive and negative changes. Thus the Knave pictures forth a vacillating, unstable, though ever-present, law. In order to more thoroughly understand what the Knave represents as applied to human life, let us understand that man has a physical and a spiritual body. He has, also, a divine spark within him which I will call his soul, or conscience, or Christ principle. It is this Christ principle that the Knaves represent. Man never sins against God or nature, himself or fellowman, except his conscience cries out in protest.

No two thoughts can be entertained at the same time, so each thought must be weighed in the balance of conscience, and this spark of divinity will always point out to us the right course: if we refuse to act according to its dictate we simply crucify Christ or kill "the widow's son," but as Christ overcame the grave and "the widow's son" was resurrected, so, after each putting aside of our conscience by us, it comes up again at each succeeding crucial point to be weighed, accepted or rejected. Thus Christ stands at the door of every human conscience knocking for admission to the human temple of the heart, which was builded without the sound of any metal tool, and on either side of the entrance thereto stand two pillars, one called strength (Man), the other beauty (Woman), and that which unites these two is the neuter or that which is of both and yet is neither one, including both within itself and yet is itself. The Knave, then, symbolizes the Christ—that principle which is not a fixture, but vibrates between the two great extremes. Christ said "I and my father are one," to humanity he pointed his finger and said, "Ye and me are brothers."

This same principle applies in the world of politics. We find the representatives of the people at the courts or throne. They are in the world of politics what the Christ is in divine law. Christ revealed to mankind the laws of God. He acted as communicator between man, the lowest, and God, the highest; so the politician of to-day represents the people at the seats of the government and to the people expresses the desire of the ruling power. He will sell out the interests of the people to the throne. He betrays the desires of the ruling power to the people and, being unstable and unreliable, he is justly called a Knave.

The Heart card is called such from its rude resemblance to that organ. As it is supposed to be the fountain from which all affection flows, the Heart is chosen as a fitting symbol of that sentiment called love; but a close study of the picture will disclose that it is a better counterfeit of a candle flame, and is really a picture of a flame of fire. To the mind of the initiate, when he sees it, this pictured flame of fire represents the name of God. We cannot but admire the wisdom of the ancient mystics who wrote the name of that principle which animates worlds, suns and systems of suns by a picture so simple of comprehension, for when we speak of God we think of that principle that names all things everywhere, in the center of the earth, in the bottom of the sea, in the heavens above; wherever life is, wherever vibration is, wherever heat is, wherever light is, there God is. Motion, gravity, all things, are full of light and these are pictured in the Heart or flame of fire. All life coming from God, the Heart is a symbol of universal life and love.

We all love to be loved, we all love to express love.

We all love life; love to express life and love; and this desire to express these principles is nicely shown and portrayed by the *attitude* assumed by the three court cards in Hearts, for it must be remembered that these court cards are symbols of laws universally operating in the mineral, vegetable and animal worlds. See how each one turns the face toward the flame of fire, showing a desire for it and longing to be one with it.

I have already shown how the Diamond is the Cross of Matter or the Cross of Christ. How beautifully it tells the story of the incarnation of the soul and of its contact with matter. There is still another interpretation to this beautiful symbol. Matter crystallizes and, as the most precious crystal on earth is the diamond, it is the most desired of all crystals. Man's earthly power is measured by his earthly wealth. He who has wealth or Diamonds has greatest power. This desire for earthly power is manifest not only in the human family but throughout the entire animal kingdom. Even in the lowest order of animal intelligence there is a manifest desire for supremacy. In the vegetable world there is the strongest tree and the largest vegetable. Notice the three court cards in the suit of Diamonds and see how fondly each one looks upon the emblem of wealth and worldly power. Do not, however, forget that the Diamond is not only an emblem of worldly power but is also the symbol of life, because within the crystal is the germ of the light—the soul from God.

The above picture is called a Club; just why, it is difficult to explain, unless because of its resemblance to the shamrock. It is a very faithful resemblance, however, of a universal plant found in the remotest corners of the earth. The first plant to make its appearance in the spring in all countries is the clover. It is also the last to disappear at the approach of winter. It is a universal summer plant and was chosen by the mystics of old to symbolize the summer time of life, since it is in the summer time of life that man gathers knowledge. The clover leaf was chosen to represent him from 12 to 30 years of age. It not only symbolizes knowledge but wisdom. The latter, a faculty of the soul, is gained only by experience. As a symbol of wisdom, therefore, the clover leaf can be said to be a picture language of the soul's growth from birth to death. Knowledge, however, is a faculty of the mind and may be gained from books, teachers and other sources. The latter belong to youth. All Kings and Queens desire to rule their kingdom wisely, hence it will be seen that the King and Queen of clubs

look with longing eyes upon the emblem of wisdom. The Knave, however, representing youth and vacillation, would hardly be expected to desire wisdom: we find the Knave of Clubs turning his face away from the emblem of wisdom; but he is shown as "knocking at the door." The spiritual nature of this card shows the Christ, or Soul of man, the living and eternal divine spirit, standing at the door of conscience knocking for admission.

So man learns by bitter experience to hearken to the voice of silence; as he does so he becomes wise and has no desire to crucify his Christ nor destroy the architect of his own temple. This wisdom, however, is never found in youth, hence the Knave of Clubs is depicted as turning his face away from the emblem of wisdom.

We have seen the Spade is the emblem of death. We all understand the Spade is the implement with which the grave is dug and after the body is deposited the same implement is used to fill in the earth. The Spade is a poor man's constant companion. With it he delves into,

turns the soil and searches in the bowels of the earth for the precious
metals.   It is an implement of labor and pictures the humble station in
life.   Associated with the Spade is the idea of labor—drudgery.

Notice the three court cards in the suit of Spades and see how
each of these crowned heads turns away from the emblem of death
and labor.   Here is a mute but universal protest against making the
journey across the silent river.   All nature rebels when asked to give
up its form of clay.   We are promised a resurrection and while knowing that death is as essential as life, yet we turn our faces away from
the death quarter.   This universal protest is beautifully symbolized
by the attitude of the three court cards in Spades.   Even the rocks cling
to their form with wonderful tenacity, and it requires years of elemental erosion to disintegrate one dead forest tree.

CHAPTER VIII.

King Solomon's Temple and the Human Body One and the Same—Diseases of Women the Result of Amorous Thoughts Directed Toward Them by Men—The Women of America Have Recognized This Law and by Resolution Have Declared Against It—Consideration of the Individual Cards—King of Diamonds—King of Spades—King of Hearts—King of Clubs—The King of Clubs Wears Upon His Breast the Ancient Badge of a Free and Accepted Mason.

Before considering the cards individually I wish to call the reader's attention to the large astrological chart in which the Archetypal Man is drawn. It will there be seen that the Heart quarter includes the head, neck and arms. This does not signify that the sentiment of love is expressed through these organs or parts of the physical body. It only means that during the months of April, May and June the sun is in that quarter and reflects or sends out the vibrations represented by the Heart suit more than by any other suit. The same can be said of each of the other three quarters. Why the sun should reflect the principle symbolized by the Heart at this time of year more than the principle symbolized by the Club we cannot answer. It simply is so.

By a further study of this chart it will be seen that the Diamond quarter includes the reins or kidneys, the sex organs and the thighs, while the Spade quarter includes the knees, calves of the legs and feet. The Archetypal Man divided by a line drawn from twenty-one degrees of Virgo to twenty-one degrees of Pisces will separate the Archetypal Man into two parts. One of these parts will include that half of the body from the navel to the feet and the other half from the navel up to the head. If now we will look upon the *human body* as the temple of God, "builded without the sound of any metal tool," we can then comprehend what is meant by the accumulation of debris referred to in the Holy Book. But people never consider the impossibility of debris accumulating during the erection of a building where there is no sawing or hammering, yet at the building of Solomon's Temple it is claimed there were many feet of accumulated debris in the face of the statement that "There was not the sound of any metal tool." Look upon this picture of the human temple and we readily comprehend that the lower half of the human body is the half that must dispose of the waste matter of the body, therefore the lower half may well be called the animal half. If man's thoughts never gravitated below the waist line or into the animal kingdom, crime, sin and sorrow would be unknown. It is the dwelling of human thoughts in the accumulated debris of the Human Temple that really calls forth the power of the Grand Master. For so long as the thoughts of man and woman are directed the one toward the other, above the waist line, just so long will images of virtue, peace and prosperity be pictured in their immortality and just so long will society be free from crime, sickness and sorrow. There is a growing belief that sexual diseases or diseases of the generative organs, especially in women, is the result of man's thought amorously directed toward those parts. Pure sexual thought is invigorating; it is adulterous thought that produces disease. The lower half of the Archetypal Man, represented by the two quarters, Diamonds and Spades, also typifies the law of involution, for it must be acknowledged that we cannot have eternal *evolution* without a corresponding eternal *involution*. Let the reader then look upon these two quarters as representing the going down of the human soul through the animal and mineral worlds and in its journey sinking lower and lower in its search after light. The human figure depicted upon this chart is bent over so that the back of the head touches the bottoms of the feet, thus constituting a human circle. If this figure should stand erect and bring the zodiacal signs up with it the sign of Aries would be at the top and the sign of Pisces at the bottom of the column or figure. Thus the human form or figure in the chart represents the whole human family, each member of the human body having its corresponding zodiacal sign, degree, etc. Each has a language portraying the lessons taught to the human soul in its contact with matter and revealing to the student or candidate the lessons of human experience.

Universal thought is fast crystalizing along these lines and we may expect the enactment of more stringent moral, if not statutory, laws.

Women, through their power of conception, are far more effective law-makers than men. When women raise their standard of what men shall be, immediately a better man is conceived, and will therefore be born.

I quote the resolutions touching this subject adopted at Washington, D. C., April, 1905, by the National Council of Women. It will be seen that already the statutes have been written and adopted, raising the standard of human thought:

Believing the progress of humanity is best furthered by improvement of the individual and that the improvement of the individual is dependent upon hereditary environment and nurture; be it

Resolved, That the perfection of the home, the institution in which heredity is fixed, the first environment of the child formed, its first nurture received, should be the object, the solicitude and the endeavor of every man and every woman who loves humanity and would serve it.

Further believing that the home can be perfected only in a society which requires equal personal chastity of men and women and confers equal responsibility upon both; therefore,

Resolved, That the National Council of Women of the United States rejoices in the organization at its fifth triennial of two committees which will focus its endeavors upon equal political liberty of women with men and equal personal purity of men with women.

Further believing that what is peculiarly needed to secure true family life is far more of plain living and high thinking on the part of the more privileged and a deeper sense of responsibility on the part of the citizen; be it further

Resolved, That in working these conditions the National Council of Women shall keep in mind that the safety and stability of the home, of society and of the state are principally dependent upon the character of their individual members.

We will now take up the construction of the individual cards, beginning with the King of Diamonds. His place, of course, is in the

quarter of Diamonds where he is supposed to be absolute monarch. The diamond is an emblem of money from a material standpoint; hence a king or ruler in this domain must stand ever ready to extend the right hand of fellowship to all people. Notice how the King extends the open hand to all comers. Sometimes, however, manufacturers of cards have represented him with the closed hand. The latter indicates the miserly king or the individual who accumulates wealth and holds it. The open hand symbolizes the liberal king who circulates his wealth. Both, however, are Kings wearing crowns—symbolic of authority. Each has a full beard, showing age, maturity, judgment, and the court robes. Each has, however, but one eye; symbolic language signifying that "man cannot serve God and Mammon." It also signifies that universal law of concentration, the key to success. "Single eye to duty."

Behind this King of money is the beheading ax. Now the language of this card is, "The right hand of fellowship to all men, but I will not spare the beheading ax to get at their money. I will sacrifice or cut off the head of my best friend to get his wealth." We see this universal law manifested every day in all walks and conditions of life. It is more apparent among the churches and fraternal orders. It has reference to the man who bedecks himself with the emblems and badges of different secret societies and because of his membership asks their business patronage. It refers to the one who, because he is the member of some church, expects the trade of his brethren. In an undertaker's office in the southern part of California the author was surprised to see almost the entire wall space covered with certificates of membership in various secret societies, showing the proprietor to be a member of about all the fraternal orders in existence. He took pains to display these certificates for business purposes only. And, dear reader, think of his calling, an undertaker; he united himself with fraternal orders that he might bury their dead. Surely here was the right hand of fellowship extended to all people and the deadly beheading ax in the other. To be a ruler, therefore, in the world of money one can have no friends aside from self; and yet one must be a friend to all in order to do business. It is said that the love of money or earthly power is the only incentive spurring man on to deeds of crime. The fact that our candidate has but one eye shows him to be imperfect and therefore not elegible to membership in some secret orders.

How am I going to give the language of this card and not give offense, for this symbol hides the truth so completely that it is almost beyond unveiling? It will be seen that the King of Spades also wears the crown, long beard, court dress and has two eyes—all of which proves the "perfect one." Our Masonic brethren have an implement called a trowel with which they spread the mortar of brotherly love, but, my brethren, there is a deeper and more sacred meaning to this, for both the Spade in the deck of cards and the Mason's trowel symbolize the same great truth; to discover this sacred secret man must go into the heart of his own tabernacle and into the recesses of his own soul. Nature, however, reveals freely her secrets to him who seeks and knocks with honesty of purpose. So let us tie a cord to a small spade or trowel and carry the same twenty-four hours suspended from our necks. As we walk among the fields and nature's bowers we will discover that at certain behests of nature man must *bury his own dead body* in mother earth. This is a beautiful symbol to teach us the lesson that man must be ever ready to meet death but never court it. The two-edged sword held in the right hand of the King of Spades is a symbol of that condition of the human soul when it is master over the three elements Earth, Water and Fire.

He has mastered one hundred and eighty degrees of the circle of infinity. He is now ready to be born into the circle of light and take his place among the selected ones. The spade, being an implement of labor and death, he who rules the world of labor must have within him those qualities of soul power that make him honored among his fellowmen and raise him from the lowest condition of human effort to the highest pinnacle of human fame and glory. Many instances of this kind are already found in the history of the United States where men, often taken from the lowest ranks of life, have been placed in the highest position in the gift of the government and the people.

Again we find the crown, two eyes, the court dress and implement of death. Again we have before us a ruler of the world. His powers, however, while twofold, must be considered this time from the standpoint of the Heart emblem. The heart being the emblem of divine love, he who would rule the world through divine love must, indeed, be willing to lay down his life under all circumstances before sacrificing his honor. See the attitude assumed by the King of Hearts: he has one hand on his breast and with the other holds aloft the unsheathed sword. The language of this sword is, "Draw me not without cause; sheath me not without honor." A king is one who dispenses favors, but this King of Hearts can only give of his kingdom —which is love or life. This card, therefore, is a symbol of that universal desire. He not only gives love but takes it away; and he who can do these things is truly divine. This is he who recognizes the Christ within himself and knows that he is the architect of his own living temple. He knows that he is one of the three model kings mentioned in connection with the building of King Solomon's Temple. He is conscious of his sonship of God and of his at-one-ment with his creator. He knows. He is.

In the King of Clubs we see the Grand Master—the Illustrious One who ever sits in the East. The source of all light and wisdom. Let us approach his sacred presence with uncovered heads and bare feet, for truly this is holy ground below and heavenly light above. This is the venerable father whose home is in that sign of the zodiac represented by the Virgin. In connection with this sign an old man is usually shown as dressing the maiden's hair. He usually has associated with him the scythe of Time. We see on the head of the King of Clubs the crown of authority. We see the same full beard of judgment and maturity, two eyes, symbolic of perfection, and the two edged sword held in the hand at "present arms." These symbolize that this one has also met death victoriously; that he, too, has overcome matter; that he has lived to manifest love divine and was not destroyed by the fires of life (symbolized by the heart) and is now entitled to wear the sacred jewel of universal wisdom. Behold on the breast of the King of Clubs a sphere—symbol of infinity.

This sphere is bisected by a horizontal line. The two halves, upper and lower, represent the two great laws in nature, male and female. The horizontal line is intersected by a perpendicular line symbolizing the descent of spirit into matter, (matter is always represented by the horizontal line and spirit by the perpendicular one), thus forming a perfect taw cross, as well as producing two triangles which interlaced become a six pointed star. When we consider that only one half of the sphere is presented to our view we see that the six pointed star would represent but half of the crown. We have therefore but to imagine the two triangles on the reverse side to give us a perfect crown of twelve points, corresponding with the twelve signs of the zodiac or the circle of infinity. Again, each of these triangles contains ninety degrees of a circle, and four of them worn on the breast show that the wearer has traveled much and found what he sought. On the horizontal and perpendicular lines are seven small spheres. These seven little spheres are the seven planets of our solar system, viz: Mercury, Venus, Mars, Jupiter, Saturn, Uranus and Neptune. These seven planets, rushing through space at such great velocity as they do, each producing a sound or note and a color, and these colors and sounds blended into one color or note, reflected to us by the sun, give us the source of all color and sound. By our musical instruments we divide this one note into its seven parts, hence, there are but seven full notes in music and but seven prismatic colors. Here, too, is the source of all the sacred sevens in the Bible: the seven stars, seven spears, seven crowns, heads, vials and cities; also the seven trumpets. The seven eyes, seven lamps, seven kings, and seven seals. If these seven little spheres refer to the stars and if, as our astrological friends say, the stars influence man, what have we to say in honor of him who by his wisdom can control his stars and wear them as an ornament to his person?

But see, from this larger sphere there seems to be a bird just taking wing or a bud just blooming. In either case it is a symbol of freedom. So let me say to all mankind: the language of the King of Clubs from an esoteric viewpoint is, "The human soul is divine and must have perfect expression. To attain this it must be buried in the elements of nature where, by experience, it overcomes the dogs of lust and passion and finally masters the dangers of darkness. Then it is free to wing its flight or come forth as the bloom from the barren stem no longer bound by the laws of matter; a perfect soul, grown in power, ready for the spiritual bride or the sacred trust of self generation. To be able to regenerate one's self at will, this constitutes wisdom, hence a wise man has power over material conditions and prepares for himself a bride which is his spiritual nature. (See Masonic emblem of Father Time and the Maiden.) He is now free from earthly conditions and takes up his abode in that heavenly home where only the pure in heart and spiritually wise can dwell. Having made the entire circuit of the celestial spheres, having ruled the world by the power of money, having overcome death as represented by the spade; having expressed divine love, healed the sick, clothed the naked and suffered as only those can suffer who have learned the lesson of charity; having grown wise by experience, his much learning and wisdom has ripened into silence, and to his knowledge he adds virtue.

The obligations imposed upon the Mason to respect the sister, mother, daughter, wife of a brother Mason is necessary to those who do not recognize their duty to their own self in the conservation of their own life forces. It is necessary that such an oath be administered to those who do not recognize *all* humanity as being members of one great fraternity.

It is necessary that men be restrained from committing the most heinous crimes by the imposition of most impressive obligations.

Men claiming to be "free and accepted" Masons so taken and received by the fraternity, are not free Masons, building temples to the honor and glory of God, but are *bound* men, and are good only because of their obligation.

The really true, free Mason is the man who recognizes and respects the virtue of every woman as that of his own sister, mother or daughter, without being sworn to do so; in whose company any woman may dwell and not be afraid.

The really true, free Mason is the man who sees in every man a brother.

The priest, who is sworn to a life of celibacy and charity is not a true son of Christ so long as he refuses to recognize in any of his priestly duties even one of God's children. He is filled with fear and ignorance, and does not go beyond his obligation to the church. He is not a freeman but is a Christian because of his fear, rather than his love, of humanity. He sees God afar off, not in his own soul. He does not hear the voice of Christ within himself.

He only hears the voice of the church, that material edifice of man, a mere symbol of the true church within himself.

The badge worn by the King of Clubs is a symbol of that soul growth that enables mankind to rule his stars by the power of the will. Of course, to rule his stars means to rule his body.

Such a person is a freeworker or builder among the elements of nature, and of course a master builder, therefore G .M. O. T. U. T.

Reform the world by reforming the individual; make him afraid of himself, rather than afraid of an unknown, unprovable deity or devil.

Change the appetite of the individual for knowledge rather than drink, and saloons will close their doors. Give to men real knowledge, not that substitute knowledge which he cannot *prove-up* by.

Teach a man how to conserve his own life force. How it can be utilized to prolong his life, increase his joy and insure him prosperity, and half the tinseled resorts of the half-world will close.

Teach a man to respect every woman as his sister, mother or daughter, and the other half will close.

Life is a religion; its altar is humanity.

CHAPTER IX.

THE KNAVE, POLITICIAN, CHRIST AND THE CONSCIENCE ALL ONE AND THE SAME—JACK OF DIAMONDS, IN SIGN OF LIBRA, SYMBOL OF THE SOUL IN ITS FIRST EMBODIMENTS; ALSO SYMBOL OF THE MASONIC CANDIDATE—JACK OF SPADES, IN SIGN CAPRICORN, SYMBOL OF THE ADVANCEMENT MADE BY THE CANDIDATE—THE ORIGIN OF THE EXPRESSION, "RIDING THE GOAT"—OVERCOMING DEATH—JACK OF HEARTS, IN SIGN ARIES, TEACHES THE SAME LESSON AS THE GRAND DEGREE OF THE ROYAL ARCH—WHEN DIVINE LOVE IS MADE A MERCANTILE COMMODITY IT BRINGS DEATH TO THE VENDOR—JACK OF CLUBS, IN SIGN CANCER, THE CANDIDATE MAKES THE GRAND DISCOVERY.

The four Knaves considered collectively represent that neuter element in nature, that which is neither positive nor negative, but vibrates between the two great extremes. In the affairs of man there are always the people and the president, or king; and there are always those who represent the people at the seat of government. These representatives also express the wishes of the king or president to the people. In the United States these middlemen are called congressmen, senators, aldermen and commissioners. They are of the people and while not of the ruling authority are yet under that authority. They wear the court robes and their interests are naturally selfish. They are the connecting link between the two ends of government. Being representatives of a vibrant or vacillating principle they are called Knaves. The reason for this is very good; these selfish individuals ever sacrifice the interests of the people to the King and in turn sell out the King to the people. They are unstable, unworthy, selfish Knaves.

Considered from a spiritual standpoint these Knaves represent the Christ principle, for did he not say, "I and my Father are one, ye and me are brothers?" Was he not always in communion with God? And yet was he not always with the people, sharing with them their joys and sorrows? And are we not taught that he is now on the right hand of God interceding for us?

In our every day lives these Knaves represent the conscience of man as it is: conscience that is ever interceding for us at the throne of the Soul, which is of God. Consequently God is ever in commune with each individual through the medium of this Christ principle. The conscience by some is called the spirit. Christ claimed nothing for himself but said He represented another; still upon His teaching is laid the foundation of the grand salvation. He was the architect of the church. The architect of King Solomon's Temple went to God daily for instructions and inspiration. The life and death of these two notable personages are nearly parallel and the Knaves or Jacks in the deck of cards are only symbols of those universal laws represented by the "Christ" of Christianity, the "widow's son" of Masonry and the "Spirit" of Humanity. No human being is ever tempted to sin against God or nature but the conscience protests: and as the conscience is set aside and the sin committed the Christ within is crucified and the architect of the temple given a felling blow. The conscience, however, can never be wholly destroyed. As Christ overcame the grave and the grand Master resuscitated so our conscience ever returns to be recognized and accepted, or rejected.

If, then these Jacks represent the soul of man we can study them individually and with much interest and profit. We will first consider the Jack of Diamonds. By reference to the large astrological chart it will be seen that the place of the Jack of Diamonds is in the House of Libra the first house of the quarter of wealth. This house has for its sign the Scales or Balance. It is the seat of the kidneys and therefore is a symbol of regeneration. The soul of man in its first contact with matter must learn to weigh, to balance, to judge. not fellow man but self.

When the soul is first baptized into the waters of gestation and comes in contact with matter it is perfect. That perfection is symbolized by the two eyes shown in the Jack of Diamonds. It is of God, and has authority which is symbolized by the crown. It is pure and innocent, as shown by the youthful and beardless face. In other words the Jack of Diamonds is a perfect type of the fitness of a candidate who knocks at the door of a Mason's temple. The working tools carried by the Jack of Diamonds consist of a cant hook carried in the hand. This is an instrument with which logs are rolled and has great power. It symbolizes that our candidate is a "builder" and while the cant hook would naturally confine building operations to log or wooden houses, it does not follow that the builder may not be a builder of houses of many other materials.

The idea of the symbol is simply to show that the candidate is a "builder;" this, of course, takes in the entire science of architecture. Why should a Mason study architecture unless it is to teach him the laws of geometry?

Other working tools are carried by the Jack of Diamonds. Upon his breast is seen a quiver filled with arrows. At first thought this would seem to suggest criminal instinct or life-taking propensities; and while such may be the purpose of the symbol, still to take life or kill the lower order of intelligence is the work of the human soul in its earlier stages of development, such as the aboriginal tribes.

But the deeper and esoteric meaning of the quiver and arrows is that man must learn to kill the memories of the past. He must let go of yesterday and take hold of to-morrow. By living in the future and thus cultivating faith the soul grows in power.

Here then in the Hall or House of Justice the soul takes up the cross of Christ, but it is ignorant of the Judases and ruffians lying in wait at every step upon the highway of life.

A quiver of arrows on the breast shows him to be a destroyer

of lower life or principles. But the cant hook held in the hand shows
him to be a hewer of wood—a builder of houses. What better illustration of the building and regenerating work of the human soul in
its contact with matter?

Christ was a destroyer of the old, a builder of the new.

This card then is a symbol of the first stages of soul growth.

We will next pay our respects to the Knave of Spades. The first

thing to attract our attention is the fact that he has but one eye, a symbol of imperfection. Now, this is the same Christ principle we saw in
the previous card, but the elements, conditions and environments are
changed. This Jack has a small growth of hair on his upper lip, showing experience and years in advance of the Jack of Diamonds.

This personage carries in his hand an hour glass, symbolizing
eternal and internal life: as the sands of one life run out the glass is
inverted, thus keeping up a perpetual stream of motion or life.

The Spade is an emblem of death. Christ asked that the cup of
death be spared him; so, too, the Jack of Spades also turns his head
away from this unwelcome visitor. The celestial sign of the zodiac
to which the Jack of Spades belongs is called Capricornus, represented
by the goat. It is the first house in the quarter of death, and since

every soul must knock at this door knowing not what is beyond the grave, the blindfolded candidate is a nice illustration of this step into the unknown; his sins are loaded on the scapegoat, hence the expression "riding the goat."

Had the soul or Christ principle, symbolized by the Knaves, successfully carried the cross of matter taken up first by the Jack of Diamonds, there would be no death to symbolize. But it failed, and presents itself at this time as imperfect, consequently not an acceptable workman in the temple of the Lord. The language of this card in the sign Capricorn is:

"I prepare my sepulchre;"

"I make my grave in the pollution of the earth;"

"I am under the shadow of death."

JACK OF HEARTS.

The Christ principle was first presented to us by the Jack of Diamonds who, representing the Perfect One, fails to carry the cross of matter; as a further expression of the Divine word he appears as the Jack of Spades; now he demands our consideration in the garb and dress of the Jack of Hearts. The first thing to consider in connection with the personality of this card is his place in the Zodiac.

He belongs to the sign Aries—which is the seventh sign from Libra counting the latter one, Scorpio two, etc. Our candidate began his first lesson in Libra; he is now found in the seventh house. This shows that he has been persevering, and, having traveled more than half-way round the circle of Infinity, he is now born anew, is raised from the dead, and as a promise that he will never again be called upon to go down into death's chamber, is given a little evergreen leaf to carry in his hand, a constant reminder of the eternal presence of a living God.

But this sprig of acacia is only a symbol of that conscious recognition of the spark of Divine fire within every one.

All of the new schools of thought, such as Mental and Divine Science, Spiritualism, Theosophy, and kindred "isms," are but class manifestations of what is here symbolized as taking place in the individual. There are many on earth to-day who are conscious of their resurrection from the spiritually dead and who have recognized this spark of Divinity within, and who know that it is their very life; when it is transferred to others by personal contact or by the spoken word, or by silent suggestion, it gives life and hope. Such workers, however, are often just what is pictured by this card—for see, he has only one eye—a symbol of imperfection. The small growth of hair on the face also indicates youth and inexperience, the beheading ax is a symbol of death. All of this shows plainly that "a little knowledge is a dangerous thing."

The language of the sprig of acacia is: "I have been in the

grave. I have triumphed over it by rising from the dead and, being re-generated by the process, I have a claim on life everlasting."

This sprig is held in the hand before the face, but the holder seems unconscious of the implement of death so close behind. He knows of his sonship with God, feels called upon to do God's work, but the ignorance of youth and innocence of childhood soon cause him to be puffed up with the idea that he is God instead of a reflector of the Divine will; this false conception proves his death by the ax. Then again, having failed to carry the cross of matter, a smouldering fire of love for worldly power, symbolized by the Diamond (money) still exists; and sometimes the fatal mistake is made in the belief that this Divine fire, or love, can be made a mercantile commodity and sold to the highest bidder. This use, or misuse, also causes death to the initiate soul.

How frequently we hear of God calling a faithful servant from one field to labor to another through the voice of an increased salary?

Again, who has not heard of that representative of God refusing to pray for a soul until the stipulated price be paid? Who, too, has not heard of the healers who would not allow the Divine fires of life to flow through their hands or minds until a satisfactory financial arrangement was made? And to you, my Masonic brother of the Royal Arch, this card is a symbol of that one who is raised from the dead to a living man; he is also that same one who in everyday walks of life sees only the letter and not the spirit. While both have been over the same road, one only is chosen and will be tried, for he sees the light.

Aries is the sign of the human head. As the head is the seat of government for the upper half of the body so, when human love finds expression through the organs of speech, mind and heart, or that portion of the body above the navel, it is life. When this love finds expression through those parts below the navel it is death.

Therefore the Jack of Hearts, being "at home" in the sign of Aries, is a symbol of the power of mind to express through the human body not only life but death. Hence, if a person thinketh on another with an impure mind, he hath already committed adultery; again if one thinketh of others with pure love and place his hands upon them they bless. The Jack of Hearts then is a symbol of the Christ principle just born and recognized; the heart a flame of fire, symbol of life, energy, love; the young face emblem of innocence; the hair on the face emblem of youth, or a little learning; the sprig of acacia, eternal life; beheading ax, death.

He faces the emblem of life showing a desire for it; but his youth, innocence and inexperience may betray him at any time to his own death. Thus, because of ignorance of God's whole law, the Christ in man is constantly being crucified and the Grand Master of God's holy temple is being eternally killed by the three ruffians—Ignorance, Fear and Selfishness. It is a wonderful responsibility to be charged with the work of carrying out the plans of the architect of the human temple. One only begins to realize it when trying to express pure Divine Love; but by repeated failures and many discouragements the soul finally comes to the Zodiacal sign Cancer (represented by the crab) and here we are introduced to the Jack of Clubs. We find he

occupies the tenth step in the spiral stairway. This number itself signifies perfection while the zodiacal animal, Crab, is an emblem of going backward; the creature goes backward in order to go forward. So, too, the Christ principle was in the beginning perfect and first found the light in the Scales of Justice (Libra). But it descended into materiality and was buried amid the rubbish of sensuality, however overcoming death finally, and being born anew amid the fires of Divine love. Being tested and tried behind the third veil and discovering that all Karmic debts of the past have been paid and all obligations to nature, man and God satisfied, the scales of darkness drop from his eyes and he now sees himself a perfect man, having two eyes, free and acceptable unto the Lord. This card then, the Jack of Clubs, symbolizes a knowledge of the law, but the fact that our friend turns his face away from the clover leaf (or Club), symbol of wisdom, shows that he is not yet ready to take a *fixed* place. He knows the law but hesitates to assume the responsibility of transferring it to others, or in any way manifesting the Divine word with which he is now possessed. Although his eyes have been opened to the truth and he has received the golden key of wisdom that unlocks all secret places, he has not recognized it when placed in his hand. The beardless face is a type of that childish simplicity that must stamp every one when all things have been made ready for an entrance into the presence of the most High One; notwithstanding we possess much knowledge we present ourselves as little children, "for of such is the kingdom of Heaven," and we "knock at the door" of the temple on high, made without the sound of any metal tool. (Observe the hand of the Jack of Clubs knocking at the door.) That he has found eternal life is beautifully symbolized by the sprig of acacia now worn in the crown, and which the Jack of Hearts carries in the hand.

I shall now leave the Christ principle, or Knaves, for a time and consider the Queens as smbolizing the negative, spiritual or intuitional nature.

CHAPTER X.

THE FOUR QUEENS—THE FLOWERS CARRIED BY THEM SYMBOLIZE
THE NINE MONTHS OF GESTATION, THE TWELVE MONTHS OF
THE YEAR, THE SIGNS OF THE ZODIAC, ETC.—QUEEN OF SPADES,
SYMBOL OF DEATH AND RESURRECTION—THE QUEEN CARD
ALSO A SYMBOL OF THE CHRIST PRINCIPLE—BIRTH OF
AMERICA THE BIRTH OF WOMAN'S FREEDOM—THE IMPORTANT
PART WOMAN IS PLAYING IN THE EVOLUTION OF THE RACE—
THE DUTY OF THE UNITED STATES—ITS RELATIONS WITH
OTHER NATIONS PROPHESIED IN THE CARDS—PHYSICAL DI-
VISIONS OF THE COUNTRY, NUMBER OF STATES, EXECU-
TIVE, JUDICIARY AND LEGISLATIVE BRANCHES SEEN AND
READ IN THE CARDS—EVEN THE DISTRICT OF COLUMBIA
SYMBOLIZED BY ONE OF THE CARDS—VISION OF AN INTERNA-
TIONAL FLAG.

Previously I have spoken of the general laws symbolized by the
Queens: I shall now only speak of the flowers, which are held in the

hands. A close observation reveals that no two of these flowers are similar, and yet all are exactly alike.

Study them closely and it will be seen that most manufacturers represent these flowers as being composed of one large square and one large circle.

The circle is a symbol of Infinity and when this circle is squared it reduces itself to the four universal elements, fire, earth, air, water.

Then there are four little squares and four little circles within the larger ones. This is a symbol of that Divine Law which requires and demands of each individual that he square his own circle, meaning that each individual has a place and a work to do, that each is given at birth a perfect rule and guide, by the use of which he can always measure himself and take his own bearings, knowing exactly how he stands with the universe.

This guide and rule is the Christ principle represented in the flower by the very small circle and square. This at first glance appears to be the calyx and, from a spiritual standpoint, that is just what is represented. Thus we find these flowers are made to represent three circles and three squares, one within the other; each is divided into four parts, making a total of twelve parts to the circles and twelve parts to the squares, corresponding with the numerical position of the Queen in each suit, her place being the Twelfth. This also corresponds with the number of signs in the Zodiac and number of months in a year.

It is easy to see the four little diamond-shaped squares on the outer edge of the flower, also the four circles that seem to form the leaves of the bloom. The sum of these four squares and circles equals eight; these eight individualities are held together by a central one, and this one plus the eight gives us the number nine, the number of months required for perfect gestation. There are four Queens; nine multiplied by four equals thirty-six: again the number of perfect gestation, or 3 plus 6 equals 9.

A Queen, then, is symbolic of the spiritual nature in man, for it is the spirit that gives life and light to the body. It is the spirit which ascends to Heaven, according to the pattern set by the great Teacher. The flower is an emblem of life and woman's function is to bring forth life; therefore only emblems of life are found associated with the Queens, with one exception, Queen of Spades; associated with her we see a lighted candle. (See Queen of Spades.) This is a beautiful way of telling in symbol the story of death and resurrection, for the Zodiacal place of the Queen of Spades is in the sign of Aquarius, represented by two wavy lines thus $\approx$. These signify the River of Death, the two lines picturing waves of water. It is the spirit that must make the journey across the River of Death, hence, the Queen being a symbol of that life which never dies, she is the proper one to carry the candle that lights the soul through the dark valley and shadow of death.

There is still another language to this card. She turns her face away from the emblem of death (the Spade), and earnestly contemplates the spiritual light within symbolized by the candle. It is woman's nature, then, to turn to God in time of trouble; instead of seeking revenge, she seeks Divine help through prayer. And now as Christmas time is with us, and we celebrate the birth of Christ, I wish to show the most startling truth yet in connection with this "little book." For this purpose I feel the need of a sub-text which shall be:

The history of the United States and its relation to the world, as read in symbols through the Deck of Cards.*

The discovery, growth and influence of this nation is the direct result of mankind's recognition of the Christ principle within him, that still small voice ever knocking at the door of each one's conscience. This voice tells all who listen that woman is as much a Divine creation as man. It also tells that woman is a ruler as well as man. But her power to rule lies in her ability to conceive life rather than to take it.

The world has always worshiped the masculine God, and we have seen by the "little book" that while the man God in nature is a destroyer the woman God in nature is a preserver.

Let us, then, with the birth of a new year and a new century, acknowledge the Mother of Life and Love in nature as well as the Father. This resolution adopted, we can take up the history of the United States as revealed in the "little book."

The discoverer of America (Columbus) listened to the little voice within and a woman furnished the means that enabled him to make the first voyage.

When Queen Isabella had heard of the New World as it appeared to Columbus, and had considered the many obstacles that stood in the way of successfully carrying out his plans, and knowing the impoverished condition of her exchecquer, she said:

"I will assume the undertaking for my own crown of Castile, and am ready to pawn my own jewels to defray the expenses of it if the funds in the treasury shall be found inadequate."

---

*This portion of this book was written several years before the publication of the present work, in a series of letters at about Christmas time.—THE AUTHOR.

The early settlement of the country was the result of man's desire to be free to express his religious opinions.

This is soon followed by THIRTEEN COLONIES, corresponding to the thirteen cards in each suit, demanding absolute freedom for all mankind, and a woman conceives an elastic banner to symbolize to the world the fact that a new principle is born, the name of which is Liberty. I say "elastic banner" for the reason that it changes every time a territory is admitted to statehood. Since the establishment of this Government, woman has been so prominent in the history of the world that it is difficult to keep pace with her. But, be it said to her honor and credit, and let it ever live in letters of eternal fire, her influence has invariably been on the side of peace and moral advancement.

Most all of the new issues tending to make man free are due to the fact that woman first gave them birth. I cannot mention all; a few will suffice. Theosophy, Blavatsky; Christian Science, Eddy; Spiritualism, Fox Sisters; the W. C. T. U., distinctly a woman's organization, an outgrowth of the woman's crusade in Ohio. Then there are many organizations of women, national and international, all having for their object the betterment of humanity. Women's clubs are springing into existence in large numbers, and their influence in our legislative bodies is growing larger each day.

The reader can follow out this line of thought and perhaps call to mind the many and important changes in our national and state laws that have been the direct result of woman's effort.

At no time, in the modern history of the world has woman been accorded such liberties and allowed to enter all vocations of industrial life so extensively as since the discovery of America.

Let us view in brief the female sex and see how unfavorably the male sex compares with her. Agrippa says:

In the first place woman is regarded as better than man, having received the better name. Man was called Adam, meaning Earth; woman, Eve, meaning Life. As much as life excels earth, woman excels man. In the order of creation, first is the incorruptible soul, then corruptible matter, beginning with minerals, herbs, trees, shrubs; then zoophites, brutes, reptiles, fishes, birds, quadrupeds; lastly two human beings. First of these the male, then the female. Then the creator rested, his work being finished. Nothing greater, nothing more beautiful than woman was conceived by the Lord.

Man was created outside the gates of paradise; woman was the first paradisaical creation. Nature respects woman's natural charms by not compelling her to suffer the humiliation of baldheadedness. Woman's purity is vouched for in the old adage that "when a woman washes she is clean;" though she wash in several waters she does not soil them, whereas if man do wash in ten waters he soils and clouds them all. It was Adam who was forbidden to eat of the fruit of the tree of knowledge. Woman was therefore created free.

St. Bernard says: Eve was chosen as a field for temptation by the devil because she was the most perfect. She erred in ignorance but man sinned knowingly. So when the Lord appeared on earth again at the dawn of the Christian era he humbled himself as man and overcame as a descendant of woman. He would not be born of man, but woman alone was the chosen vessel and medium. She alone was considered fit to be a parent of the Divinity.

They were women who first met the Lord after His death; He honored them by making His appearance first to them.

No persecution or heresy in the church ever began with woman.

They were men who betrayed, sold, bought, accused, condemned, mocked and cruicified the Lord. Women were at the foot of the cross and they were at the sepulchre.

The Virgin Mary is the chief prop of the church.

Adam, fresh from the creative hands, fell an easy captive to woman's charms.

Samson's strength failed him in the presence of a woman.

Solomon was wise, but a woman deceived him.

Job was patient until a woman disturbed it.

It was Peter the favorite who was, by woman, made to deny his Lord.

Even the wickedness of woman is in the eyes of the Lord many times preferable to the virtues of the men.

Rachel was praised for deceiving her father, and Rebecca because she obtained fraudulently Jacob's benediction.

We die in the seed of Adam and live in the seed of Eve.

The first bigamists, drunkards and tyrants were men. The history of the world is red with the blood of men, and our prisons are filled with men.

Abraham was told to hearken to the voice of Sarah his wife.

The scientific and learned doctor is often discomfited and put to flight by the ignorant midwife.

The wise astrologers of old, as "shepherds," saw by the configurations of the heavens that a Savior was to visit the earth but He, the Savior, was conceived of woman, and during His ministry woman was first to be forgiven of her sins.

That man regards woman as his superior is shown by the deference extended her when meeting on the street. He always gives her the right of way. He worships at her shrine and bedecks her noble body with the finest of raiment and jewels.

It was St. Paul who said: "Wives, be subject to your husbands," but it must not have been a Divine Law he was speaking of, for he also said: "In Christ there is neither male nor female but a new creature."

The United States as a member of the family of nations has a duty to perform—that duty is prophesied and symbolized by the deck of cards. The signs of the times already point to the fulfillment of the prophesy.

The prophesy is that universal peace shall come to the civilized world; that wars shall give way to reason (through arbitration).

With the disappearance of war, woman's sphere of activity and usefulness will be equal to that of man. Through the intuitional and inspirational nature of woman, man is being more and more psychically developed; as his inner nature becomes awakened, and he becomes more open to inspiration his inventive genius waxes more alert. As a result of this the agencies of war become more and more destructive: finally the nations of earth will not dare to go to war. Even now man's inventive genius has enabled him to almost annihilate distance. Balloons, telephones, wireless telegraphy, torpedoes, hand granades, smokeless powder, cannon with a range of twenty-five miles, portable railroads and armored trains, all, combine to make war, even now, most horrible to contemplate. Should the arts and sciences advance during the next fifty years in a corresponding ratio with that made during the past fifty years, it is not difficult to see why nations would seek arbitration rather than war.

In the future the greatest diplomat will be the greatest warrior. "Blessed be the peacemaker." The world is rapidly growing too small for war.

The United States is built upon a number plan and if there be any true science at all it must be the science of numbers.

Christ was the thirteenth one.

He was the embodiment of the principle of freedom. He said He came to set the world free, to establish freedom.

The United States is formed or established on the Christ principle. It therefore becomes the duty of the United States to carry the lighted torch of liberty to the nations of the earth; not by imposing upon other nations American customs, but by example, and the first great example is the liberty and equality of woman—even now an accomplished fact in the United States.

Already the proclamation has been made in symbol by the colossal female statue carrying the lighted torch of liberty at the entrance to New York harbor, the principal port of the country.

That the American people have recognized the universal mother principle and placed it above all other things dear is shown by the fact that all gold and silver money bears the likeness of an *American woman*.

This image is not that of any particular woman, made to do honor to any particular time or administration. It is free from personal exaltation: it is an image of perfect womanhood as conceived by the American people.

The likeness is surrounded forever by the thirteen original stars, and across her brow they have written the word "Liberty."

Man's spiritual nature is said to be feminine; American man has unconsciously placed upon his money a picture of his spiritual nature.

Upon the reverse side he has engraved an eagle. This again is an unconscious recognition of the spiritual nature, for while the eagle is called the "king of birds," and "king of the air," still no male eagles are ever found; they are all females. (So claimed by Agrippa.)

Thus upon man's earthly God (money) has he engraved a picture of his spiritual God (woman); to further show his faith in the freedom of the spirit he has caused to be graven a symbol of freedom in the "king of the air" (eagle).

The physical make-up and divisions of the United States correspond with the physical make-up and divisions of the deck of cards.

The United States is divided into two great parts or halves by the Mississippi river, corresponding to the two colors in cards. The eastern half of the United States is again divided by the Ohio river and the western half by the Missouri river, thus producing four quarters, corresponding to the four suits. Besides these physical divisions the country has been mentally divided, the North against the South, the West against the East. The latter on the money question, the former on the slavery issue. Of course, both these questions at present seem to have been settled and the country is apparently a unit, still no one can tell what day a question may arise causing the country to take sides again.

We started with thirteen states corresponding to the thirteen cards in each suit. We have grown to forty-five (with three knocking at the door): There will be fifty-two before the perfect fulfillment of the law, before the object of the birth of the United States will be fully realized and known.

When Liberty's child, Kansas, asked to be adopted, the unholy and unclean thing, slavery, had to be expunged. Kansas may be said to have been the cause of the death of slavery in the United States.

Later, as though to amend any wrongs that may have been committed on her account, she was first to give to woman freedom and equality with man through the ballot.

Thus did Liberty, in giving birth to Kansas, rid herself of the obnoxious disease. Almost the first act of the child in its early adolescence was to give back to mother Liberty her own freedom. It was Kansas that first adopted the prohibition law; a movement which was and is distinctively of woman.

The Government of the United States is divided into three heads, Executive, Judiciary, Legislative. Each department is authoritative and distinct, yet they are interdependent.

Corresponding with the three court cards in each suit. Thus the King is the superior card in each suit. He is the ruler, and by reason of the weapons carried in his hand, which indicate he is a ruler by might. He corresponds with the President or Executive.

The Queen in each suit is also a ruler, as shown by her crown, but her ruling power is indicated by the flower carried in the hand. It is a symbol that her power to rule lies in her power to conceive, thus her rulings or conquests are peaceful. The Queens correspond with the

Judiciary. The Legislative body represents that neutral quality repre-sented by the Jacks or Knaves. The members of the legislature come direct from the people. They are of the people. They are also the ad-visors and counsellors of the President. They communicate to the people the wishes of the president. They inform the president of the desires of the people.

A selfish lot they are, not hesitating to sell out the president to the people, or vice versa. Unstable, unreliable, vacillating: because of this they are *Knaves*.

The District of Columbia is a part of the United States and the seat of Government; yet it is not a state and takes no part in politics, none of its citizens ever voting. It is presided over by three commis-sioners, again corresponding with the three court cards in each suit.

The streets and avenues of Washington City lead to all points of the compass.

Whatever the party in power is, that also Washington is.

She changes her citizenship, therefore her complexion, with each changing administration. She is the constant ruler, yet ever changing to suit the trumps.

The District of Columbia is to the United States what the Joker is to the Deck of Cards. And while the Joker may be said to be a recent addition to the pack, I reply it is no more recent than the intro-duction of the United States into the Gallery of Nations; one is as young as the other.

And as I pen these lines I see, as in a vision, a new universal flag with a white field, emblem of purity. It has upon it a red heart, em-blem of Love, and a green clover leaf, emblem of wisdom. The lan-guage of this banner is "Virtue expressed in Love, peace and wisdom."

And I hear a voice saying: "Any nation that shall adopt this flag and live its principles shall have eternal life."

Now let me refer to the text: "It shall be in thy mouth sweet as honey, and in thy belly bitter."

The deck of cards has for centuries been in the world's mouth. And it has been sweet because it has been used for a plaything—a means of pleasure, an instrument of vice. But once let man digest it by becoming acquainted with the laws it symbolizes; let man "eat it up" and become wise in its teachings and then it does, indeed, become bitter, because it forces one to walk in the straight and narrow path.

The American Flag may some day have fifty-two stars, and woman may some day be man's equal, provided the law of the Lord is perfect.

As has been pointed out, the duty of the United States and its relation to the balance of the world is that of "light bearer," "peace maker," "mediator," as that prophecy is written in the sacred book of 52.

We are a nation of Masons, of Christians, at the present free. Are we to be "taken" and "accepted' as such by the grand architect of the Universal temple?

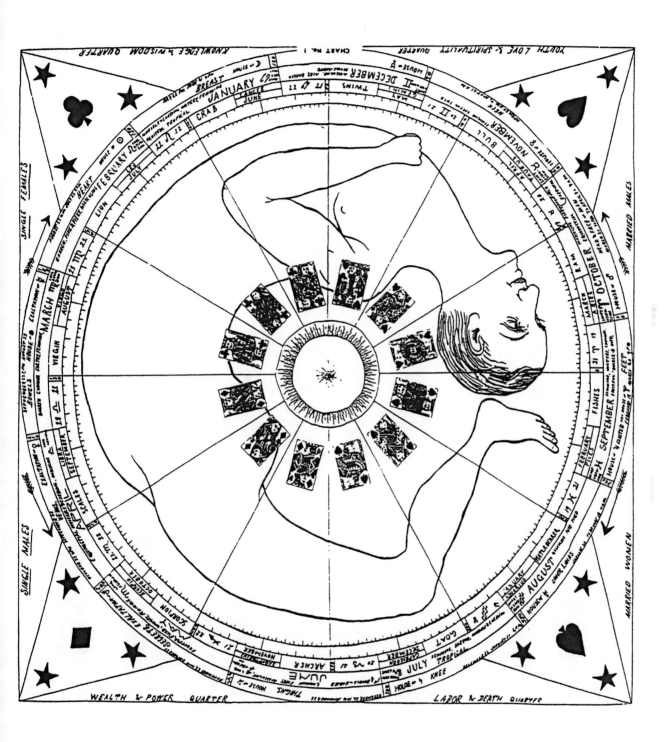

PART VI.

MORE DISCLOSURES AND
GRAND DISCOVERIES. THE
LITTLE BOOK STILL HOLDS
OUR ATTENTION AND BY
THE AID OF THE GRAND
MAN OF THE UNIVERSE
WE OPEN TO VIEW NEW
AND UNHEARD-OF USES
FOR THE SACRED EMBLEMS

PART SIX.

By reference to Chart No. 1,* of which Part VI is explanatory, it will be seen that the names of the months are repeated in the different circles. The only circle the reader will consider, however, is that wherein the name of the month is written in the LARGEST TYPE. For instance, March and August appear in the sign Virgo. This simply means that on the first day of March the earth is in the sign Virgo ten degrees.

Each degree is indicated by a short radial line on the inside of the inner circle. During the month of March the world passes through Virgo and into Libra ten degrees. Of course the sun, being opposite to the earth, would appear in the signs of Pisces and Aries, therefore the large type has reference to the location of the EARTH for any day in the year; the small type locates the SUN for the same period. Thus it will be seen by those having a knowledge of the science of astrology that the two systems, Geocentric and Heliocentric, are embraced. The former assumes the Earth to be the center of the universe, the latter the Sun.

The chart was made for class work in the study of Symbolism and contains much that cannot possibly be explained in book form. The reader is requested, however, to study the chart in connection with this chapter in order to get the full benefit of the author's meaning.

*Several orthographic errors appear in the Chart; unavoidable lack of time prevented their correction for use in the present edition.—AUTHOR.

CHAPTER XI.

THE GRAND ARCHETYPAL MAN—THE FOUR SUITS CO-ORDINATE
WITH THE FOUR ELEMENTS, FIRE, EARTH, AIR AND WATER—
GROWTH AND DEVELOPMENT OF OUR BODIES SHOWN TO BE THE
RESULT OF PLANETARY INFLUENCE—BY THE CHART EVERY ONE
CAN SEE THE NATURE OF HIS CROSS—IT IS A PICTURE OF
THE MASONIC GRAND LODGE OR KING SOLOMON'S TEMPLE—THE
CANDIDATE IS SYMBOLIZED BY THE JACK OF DIAMONDS IN THE
SIGN LIBRA, QUARTER OF WEALTH—THE TRAMP AND THE
MILLIONAIRE—THE KIDNEYS BRAINS OF SEXATION—THE TWO
PILLARS OF THE TEMPLE.

EXPLANATION OF CHART.

To the reader versed in astrological science or one having even a
"reading knowledge," much of this chart will be self-explanatory.

The Mason will find but little, at first glance, to remind him of
the teaching of Masonry, yet this chart is a picture of the universal
temple, telling the same story and revealing the same laws as are revealed to the candidate in his journey from the lowest to the highest
degrees.

The Christian will perhaps be slow to admit that the Signs of the
Zodiac and the Deck of Cards have anything to do with the "revealed
plan of salvation." Nevertheless, the whole story of the Bible from
beginning to end is included in this chart.

It is not the author's desire to explain it from any standpoint other than that of Masonry.

The circle is, of course, a symbol of Infinity; it is symbolic of that great circle including our sun and the solar universe.

The four emblems at the corners—Heart, Club, Diamond and Spade—are the symbols of the four universal elements, Fire, Air, Earth and Water. By the influence of the planets one upon the other within this universal circle, causing these four elements to chemicalize and commingle, our bodies are formed. In other words, our bodies are formed by, or rather are the result of, planetary influence and are composed of the four elements.

As proof that our bodies are the result of planetary influence it is only necessary to call the reader's attention to the changes recorded in the human body as a result of planetary change. Follow the growth of the body from time of conception.

At the end of one revolution of the moon around the earth or, twenty-seven days from conception, certain conditions prevail, cords and tendons are united and menstration ceases. Upon the eighty-seventh day, or when Mercury has made one revolution around the sun, which is the ninety day period, it is impossible to separate the foetus from the mother; for the Lord hath "sealed" and "they whom the Lord hath sealed let no man put asunder."

One revolution of Mercury is equal to *three* of the moon and when the moon has made seven revolutions around the earth the planet Venus has made one; in other words we are sealed by the planet of beauty and love (Venus), and it is under the harmonious influences of this planet that our bodies are perfected and many are born at the seventh month, this being the month of perfection. The full period of gestation, however, requires nine revolutions of the moon or three revolutions of Mercury, which equal certain perfect fractional parts of revolutions of the larger planets, dating from the time when we are born into the world to take up the cross of matter on the *five points of contact.*

At this period the earth, however, has made but three-fourths of its journey around the sun: when it has completed its circle (occurring about the third month after birth), the moon has made thirteen circuits around the earth, Mercury has made four around the sun, and Venus has almost completed its second circuit around the sun. Of course all the larger planets have progressed a certain number of degrees through the various signs of the Zodiac.

About one year from birth we ripen under the influence of Mars; or as that planet does not complete its circuit around the sun (from the time of our conception) until we are about one year old, we may be said to be sealed by him at that time: his influence is manifested by the "intelligence" displayed, and we begin to measure distance by reaching out for things and in many ways exhibiting reason.

The next planet we ripen under or are "sealed" by is old Jupiter, who requires twelve of our years to go around the sun once. He lingers one year in each of the twelve signs of the Zodiac, and when he completes his journey around the sun and returns to the point whence he started when we were conceived we respond to that return by becoming competent or arriving at the age of puberty.

Saturn or Satan requires twenty-nine years, or about that, to complete one circuit around the sun. Saturn is a spiritualizing planet: his influence is upon the spiritual rather than the physical nature, and our physical bodies stop growing at about that time of life, and our minds turn into such channels as cause us to contemplate the future state. Extraordinary experiences generally accompany the ripening influences of this planet: sickness, accidents, marriage, childbirth, journeys, divorces, etc. Saturn is called the God of Death and as it is Saturn's influence which causes the growth of the body to cease and the spiritual nature to awaken it does not require very strong imagination to discover why Saturn should be called an evil planet, and also reveal the origin of his Satanic Majesty.

At about the twenty-ninth year the physical body dies (metaphorically speaking) and the spiritual man is born or awakened.

Many people experience religion at this time or have a decided change of religious faith or in some manner are brought to consider life from a new viewpoint.

The next planet to seal us with the stamp of fate is Herschel or Uranus whose year is equal to eighty-four of ours: he consumes eighty-four of our years in girdling the sun once.

He remains seven years in each of the twelve signs of the Zodiac.

The influence of Uranus is also spiritual; the work begun by Saturn in our twenty-ninth year is supposed to be finished by Uranus in our eighty-fourth year. His ripening influence is generally most marked; second sight, new teeth, second growth of hair and many other noticeable changes mark his completed journey around the sun.

Neptune, the outer sentinel of our solar system, whose year or circuit around the sun is equal to one hundred and sixty-four of our years, is also a great spiritualizer; he *never fails* to complete the work of spiritualizing begun by Saturn.

Very marked changes take place in both men and women at the forty-second year, and again in the forty-ninth. These changes, no doubt, are results of planetary combinations, as the forty-second year is the half of a Uranian year and a fourth of a Neptunian year.

These observations, being only general in character, are given here to indicate to the student a line of thought which, if followed, will lead to rich discoveries.

The human figure drawn within the circle is the Archetypal Man, or man of the universe, in the image of whom we are all made.

If the reader will refer to the chart and find the month in which he was born, then count the lines on the inside circle, one for each day, he can by this means ascertain in just what part of the Grand Solar Man the "Earth" was at the time of his birth. Then by counting back nine months he will see in what part of the Grand Man conception took place. The sun and earth *appear* to be opposite each other, therefore, knowing where the earth was at birth, the sun must have been in exactly the opposite sign. Hence if one will locate the *earth at conception and birth* on the chart, then draw a line to the opposite sign (the location of the sun), he will see just what is the nature of the *cross* with which he was laden at birth.

To illustrate: We will say a person is born September 30. The Earth was in Aries (where the Jack of Hearts is) 10 degrees. The sun was, of course, in the sign of Libra (where the Jack of Diamonds is). Counting backward nine months the earth would be in Cancer (Jack of Clubs) about ten degrees, and the sun in Capricorn (Jack of Spades).

If the sun was in the house of Capricorn at time of conception and if the sun be the source of all light and life then Capricorn furnished the soul that was baptized into the waters of gestation in the house of Cancer.   That which was conceived, then, in Cancer was brought forth nine months afterward in the sign of Aries.

Capricorn furnishes the soul, from the sun; Cancer furnishes the matrix, the Earth; Aries furnishes the completed body, the Earth; Libra blesses the work because the sun is in Libra at the time the first breath is drawn; "and the Lord blesses everything and calls it good."

Masonry, as a school, teaches the law of the soul.   The Masonic candidate in all his initiations imitates the soul.   The soul being from Heaven or God is sexless and innocent of earth's experience.

It is perfect and has power and dominion over matter.

The journey of the soul in its contact with matter is beautifully delineated by the four Jacks in the chart.   As the Jacks are symbols of the neutral quality it will be seen they fitly typify the soul.

The chart taken as a whole is a symbol of King Solomon's temple, the entrance being at Libra, the Scales, in the quarter of Diamonds, and the candidate is symbolized by the Jack of Diamonds, who is per-

fect in body, his perfection being symbolized by the two eyes.   He is of God and has authority, manifested by the crown.   His innocence and inexperience are shown by the beardless face. He carries in his hand a cant hook with which he rolls the logs and heavy timbers together, thus proving him to be a "builder." Upon his breast he carries a quiver of arrows, symbolic of destruction; in other words the quiver of arrows symbolizes that the soul, the traveler or candidate, must depend upon the country through which he is sojourning for sustenance. It also means that we are to let go of yesterday as being forever dead, while the cant hook is a symbol of hope and faith in the future.

God sometimes tries our faith by taking from us all our accumulated wealth. It requires a stout heart to spend the last cent.

The speculator on change or the gambler, venturing his last dollar on a single deal, manifests more faith in humanity, more faith in God, more faith in himself; is by far a braver man and stands nearer to God, than the hypocritical Christian who serves the devil six days and God one, or the Mason who takes the degrees and covers himself with jewels, yet sees in them only an opportunity to further his own personal ends.

The tramp internally is a millionaire, for he is satisfied.

The millionaire internally is a tramp, for he is filled with fear and vexation of spirit.

The candidate enters the temple at the House of Libra, symbolized by the Balances. These are metallic and have no feelings of sympathy or favoritism. They weigh for the rich and the poor alike.

They are the symbol of universal justice, that "as a man soweth so shall he reap." They teach the lesson that there are no *honorary members* in heaven or hell; that both places or conditions are filled with souls who have worked their way there and earned their just reward. They teach the candidate that he must weigh himself in dealings with mankind; instead of judging his neighbor he is to judge himself.

Our candidate enters the temple through that portion of the Grand Man known as the kidneys, the brains of sexation.

They might be likened to the two pillars at the entrance of Solomon's temple, called strength and beauty, male and female, or father and mother.

The Diamond (which is the cross of matter folded up as is shown in another chapter,) is taken on by the soul and *in the Diamond quarter* the soul lingers for ages, having many and repeated lives.

It learns how to govern matter by the power of will. It learns how to wisely and justly use earthly power coming as a result of large landed possessions, as those of the nobility.

It learns how to wisely use money and to justly dispense the favors resulting from the possession of great wealth.

It learns that from the soul which has much much is expected.

CHAPTER XII.

JACK OF SPADES, SIGN CAPRICORN, QUARTER OF DEATH—THE CAN-
DIDATE HAS LOST HIS PERFECTION—LEARNS THE LESSON OF
COMPENSATION—THE SCAPEGOAT—IT IS IN THIS QUARTER
THE SOUL MEETS AND OVERCOMES DEATH.

After mastering the quarter of Diamonds our candidate next appears as the Jack of Spades in the quarter of Death or Spades.

In his contact with matter he has lost original perfection and he
now appears imperfect, which is symbolized by the *one eye*.

He still has divine authority—shown by the crown. He is still
young and inexperienced—shown by the youthful face. The mustache,
though, shows added experience. He realizes fully that he is to learn
the lesson of death, yet turns his face from the emblem of death, earnestly contemplating an hour glass held in the hand. He watches the
sands run from one end to the other, a symbol that as the sands of
one life run out the glass is inverted and the same sands and the same
life are again set in motion. He contemplates nature, observing that

season follows season; that the trees do not suffer when shedding their leaves; that the earth gives abundantly year after year, but that she demands a return of every morsel given. He is taught that all life is of God and that God too demands a complete return of all He hath given.

In the first house of the quarter of spades is that portion of the anatomy of the Grand Man called the knees. These are the feet of prayer and are symbols of humility and meekness. When the soul enters the portals of death he comes in fear and trembling, metaphorically, on bended knees.

When the messenger of death makes his appearance, the soul leaves the sins of the body behind, entering blindfold, so to speak, into the unknown.

The Goat of Capricorn is made the "scapegoat"; the candidate is said to ride the goat, which is to say, when a candidate enters a Mason's lodge he dies to the world and rides the goat of initiation into the unknown mysteries which must forever be as sacred to him as death.

In the quarter of death symbolized by the Spade (Acorn) the candidate soul learns the great grand lesson that man has a triune nature: Spirit, soul and body; that the acorn as a symbol teaches that the outer shell corresponds with the outer body; that the kernel, or meat, corresponds with the spirit; that the germ corresponds with the soul; that as we study the acorn we learn that it must die from the parent tree, be buried in the cold black earth, where it rots, disintegrates and decays in order that the soul of it may come forth a new tree.

Our candidate soul after many and repeated expressions finally learns to meet death fearlessly and with at least some degree of knowledge of what lies beyond the grave. He knows that death does not end all, that the change called death is only a change, not a destruction or annihilation, that the veil between the two worlds is not altogether opaque.

Having become a master of this quarter he can with a feeling of truth say, "I have died and been buried and having overcome the grave am now entitled to everlasting life."

Death has no more terrors and our candidate, instead of being afraid of death, faces it with that bravery and candor only a fearless soul can know. The bravery is a result of knowledge, rather than fanaticism or blind faith, and gives to the possessor that respect for life which wisdom brings. He regards life in whatever form as Divine and entitled to liberty to express itself to the fullest extent of its opportunity.

Even the most venomous reptile to him is entitled to liberty and freedom of expression. He sees God in everything.

Laws are unnecessary to protect life at his hand: he is a law unto himself. As Emerson says:

"He needs no army, fort or navy—he loves men too well; no bribe, or feast, or palace, to draw friends to him; no vantage ground, no favorable circumstance. He needs no library, for he has not done thinking; no church, for he is a prophet; no statute book, for he is the lawgiver; no money, for he is value; no road, for he is at home wherever he is; no experience, for the life of the creator shoots through him and looks from his eyes."

CHAPTER XIII.

Jack of Hearts in Quarter of Love, Sign Aries—The Candi-
date Is Still Imperfect—Having Overcome Death He Is
Now Taught the Lesson of the Evergreen Leaf—He
Learns to Walk With God—The Debris of Solomon's
Temple, Human Thought—The Discovery and Raising of
the Grand Master by the Candidate Himself—The Three
"J"s.

Having descended from the House of Libra down through the
quarter of Death (Spades) covering six degrees, or one half of the
grand circle, our candidate now appears as the Jack of Hearts in the
sign Aries of the heart quarter or quarter of love.

He is still struggling with his selfish nature, is more or less imperfect, symbolized by the *one eye.* His divine power is still at his
command, shown by the royal crown. He is still a searcher after light
and a student willing to learn, manifested by the youthful face. His

innocence is also shown by the beardless face. He faces the emblem of love, showing a desire to manifest that divine gift, but as the heart is really a picture of a flame of fire it is also a symbol of the soul being led by the light within, the fire of conscience.

Our candidate has in his hand a sprig of acacia or evergreen leaf, a symbol of eternal life. This is given for his contemplation after the trying ordeal of passing through the quarter of Death. It is to remind him of the eternity of life and to be a mute witness of the eternal truth that to die is to live and to live is to die, and lest our candidate forget that "in the midst of life we are in death," he has associated with him a beheading-ax. It is behind him, so he never knows when his life's journey may be cut short.

A Savior or Christ are the duties of life imposed upon a soul that would express all that which is symbolized by the Jack of Hearts in this quarter; for he must express divine love consciously. To be more explicit, the soul here pictured is to heal the nations by the power of the spoken word. This is that power of love which is being expressed by hundreds and thousands in the world to-day; it is called Magnetism, Divine Science, Christian Science, Mesmerism, Hypnotism and Suggestion. All this, reduced to one creed, means "the power to speak the truth consciously."

The sprig of acacia is a promise to him who will use this divine power for good of everlasting life; he who uses his power for evil, intentionally, shall lose his life, as symbolized by the beheading-ax.

Since starting on his journey in the sign Libra our candidate has passed six of the great signs of the Zodiac, has taken *six* degrees, and is now in the *seventh*. He descended through the six signs covering the animal man, at the beginning of which are the kidneys, said to be the brains of procreation.

There is a legend in connection with the building of King Solomon's temple to the effect that the architect of the temple was attacked by three ruffians and accidentally killed and that the body was buried in the "debris," the latter being very deep. But few readers of the legend ever stop to consider the utter impossibility of debris accumulating where there is not the sound of any metal tool. They do not stop to reason that if there is no sawing, carving, splitting and hewing, there cannot possibly be any accumulation of *debris*.

The debris referred to, then, must be of a nature different from that we are wont to ascribe to that term.

The legend beautifully hides the truth and proves abundantly the wisdom of those ancient mystics who sought by means of legends and pictures to keep the light of truth forever burning on the altars of human brotherhood.

As the kidneys are the brains of procreation it is through them that all human desire must find expression, and, as man's hopes, prayers and ambitions are born in his progeny, it is plain to see how that portion of the human anatomy from the kidneys down to the feet can be likened to the debris of a building, for so long as human thought is held *above the waist line* it is not a maker of waste or animal matter.

Adulteration does not consist in a union of the sexes but rather in the action of adulterated thought upon matter. Impure or adulterated thoughts, when born into flesh and blood, produce imperfect, sinful specimens of humanity.

The creative power of the soul can be used for evil as well as for good, but evil can only be discovered from the standpoint of good and vice versa. The spirit of lies can only express itself *truthfully* as a lie.

The world of matter, because of its changefulness and instability of form, is not the everlasting truth, and when the soul becomes *entangled*, as it were, in its meshes it may be said to "be buried in the debris of the temple." The legend, however, goes on to state that the architect was "discovered" and *raised* from the supposed dead state. This discovery and raising from the dead is nicely symbolized by the Jack of Hearts in the sign Aries, it being the seventh sign from Libra counting the latter one, Taurus two, and Saggitarius three.

The "discovery" is made by the candidate himself when, finding himself in the quarter of divine love, symbolized by the heart, and realizing that he has successfully passed through the quarter of Death, has actually died, been buried, and still lives, he awakens to the grand realization that in order to express divine love he must see in every man that same spark of divine fire he knows shines within himself.

He makes the "discovery" that he is himself an expression of the word: that every human being has the same source as himself, that each and every soul is a worker in the universal temple. He makes the "discovery" that every human soul is a brother or sister journeying toward the same goal, each following the light within according to the dictates of his own conscience; each actuated by the same divine fire and, whether the results of their actions be for *right or wrong*, they are still entitled to brotherly love which includes forgiveness.

Hmanity reads the story of Christ and admires the example set.

Doctors of Divinity say that He set the pattern of salvation, but who among poor humanity can forgive the ordinary criminal? Much less if nailed to the cross could they from their innermost soul say, "Father, forgive them, for they know not what they do?"

It is in this seventh degree or first house in the quarter of Love that the Jack of Hearts truly pictures forth the lesson which man must discover for himself that he is his own dear Savior, and in order to save himself he must forgive sin wherever it may exist; but first of all, before he can forgive sin in others, he must know his own sins have been forgiven, and this forgiveness of his sins is symbolized by the sprig of acacia. Having purified himself by passing through the quarter of death and having come into a conscious realization of his son-ship of God, he is now prepared to become a co-worker with God.

To do God's will then in the forgiveness of sin is the grand lesson of this combined symbol.

The three ruffians spoken of in the legend as having killed the architect are FEAR, IGNORANCE and SELFISHNESS, sometimes referred to as the three "J"s.

These three principles, when given full expression, will so encase the soul in quagmires of matter as to make it necessary that a Christ come to the rescue.

Through fear that the needs of to-morrow will not be supplied, man becomes selfish and distrustful, tyrannical and inhuman, forgetting the rights of his fellow man and even perjuring his own soul in his mad desire to gratify his selfish nature.

Because of his ignorance of the laws of his own being he suffers sickness and deformities and dies prematurely.

Because of these three ruffians human laws are necessary.

Lawmakers do not enact laws for their own personal government but for the government of their fellowman. The candidate for office never asks for the suffrages of his constituents in order that he may enact laws for himself. It is his neighbor he wishes to control, and the root of his desires is in one or all of the three ruffians.

Statutes are not made for statute makers.

Our candidate has made the grand discovery that he has eternal life and walks with God, is a co-worker of God, knowing the law of good and evil. Still he must suffer the humiliation of having the finger of scorn pointed at him and hear the ignorant rabble shouting "He saved others, himself he cannot save."

CHAPTER XIV.

Jack of Clubs, Quarter of Wisdom, Sign Cancer—The Candidate Takes the Degree of Perfection and Is Crowned With Life Everlasting—The True Lesson of the Cable Tow Is Revealed—The Legend of Osiris and Isis—The Zodiacal Sign of the Crab (Cancer) a Symbol Teaching the Same Lesson as the Cable Tow—The Candidate Soul Discovers and Lays Hold of His Own Heart—He Becomes the Word—An Ancient Badge of a Free and Accepted Mason.

Having descended through the "debris" of the temple of human thought and having been raised from the dead, he now starts on the upward journey through the quarter of love (Hearts), having for his goal the House or degree of Cancer, symbolized by the Crab in the quarter of Clubs (wisdom).

Here our candidate, as the Jack of Clubs, shows that he has

profited by his experiences and is now perfect, having discovered that which he sought. His perfection is symbolized by the two eyes.

He has returned to his pristine innocence, purity and virtue, symbolized by the youthful and beardless face. He is of God and still has authority, shown by the court crown. No longer, however, is life a mystery, for he wears the sprig of evergreen in his crown, indicating he has been crowned with life everlasting.

To the sum of all his experiences and, notwithstanding he is consciously walking with God and doing God's will, he still desires more light, and stands at the door of the temple knocking for admittance into those recesses where can be found the Jewel of precious knowledge he now realizes has been left behind. The face is turned away from the (Club) emblem of knowledge, this attitude showing that the past as well as the future holds its lessons of worth. In this degree our candidate discovers the real lesson taught by the Cable Tow. He now sees that it has grown longer and larger each succeeding degree.

The Cable Tow. is a symbol of the one connecting ray of remembrance that furnishes a means by which may be registered the many trials and tribulations of the soul in its contact with mater.

Thus we are told in the Egyptian sacred legend that Osiris (the sun) was slain by Typhon, a gigantic monster typical of darkness and the evil power of nature. The body was placed in a chest, thrown into the River Nile and swept out to sea.

Isis (the moon) ransacks the whole earth in search of the body which she finally finds horribly mutilated. She joins the severed parts and raises him to life again. The legend is a beautiful symbol beautifully hiding the truth: The four elements are four great solvents: water will in time reduce all material forms to their atomic construction. Animal bodies, when buried in the earth, soon rot and pass back to their former chemical properties, to be re-embodied into other forms, but the soul of man, being neither positive nor negative, is immune from the powers of attraction and repulsion and cannot, therefore, be dissolved by the elements. Even the element, fire, has no effect on the soul. The vibrations of soul are many millions times greater than the vibrations of fire, even of the degree of heat necessary to melt metals.

The author has asked many Masons and searched many publications for a true definition of the Cable Tow, but has found no one who recognizes it as teaching the Law of Re-embodiment or Re-incarnation. Each strand of the Cable Tow symbolizes a life or expression of the soul, each expression binding the soul to that particular epoch. Each span of life (even though it may be an hundred years) is but a moment in the eternity of time, and each life is so impinged upon the future as to be a part of it, the same as each hour of the day is but a small fraction of the whole; as each day may be viewed in its entirety from any one hour, so may the life of a soul be viewed in its entirety— when the soul has arrived at that degree of unfoldment here symbolized by the Jack of Clubs in the sign of the Crab.

The esoteric meaning of this sign of the Zodiac is quite significant. The crab is so constructed that it goes forward or backward with equal agility. Indeed, its make-up is such that it matters not in what direction it goes it is always *forward*. It is a symbol of that degree of unfoldment which must come to every soul when it sees for a certainty the *infinite past and the eternal future*. A condition arrived at which will permit the candidate soul to exclaim knowingly: "Before Abraham was I am." It comes into a definite and conscious realization of the fact that time is a measurement of moving bodies and has no place in eternity; that in the realm of soul there is no time, and that all the eternities are merged into *Now*.

The candidate soul learns the lesson of purpose and finds that "that which is to be will be and that which has been was to be."

The Cable Tow, he discovers, is only a symbol of the law of Karma, and he rejoices in the conscious return into at-one-ment with God or himself. He now sees himself from his beginning. And as he looks back over the endless Cable Tow, he sees that its other end merges into the immediate future; then, contemplating the future or scrutinizing his Cable Tow stretching before him, he discovers it to be a circle, every portion of which is a beginning and ending in himself.

Having now made the discovery within himself of that which he has sought, he is no longer satisfied with "substitute" knowledge.

He now knows the truth regarding his own being. He has the Key that will unlock for him the mysteries of the future—and the vaults of the dead past. No one has given him this key; he has discovered it for himself, for it is himself. No one could give it.

He sees how valuable every experience has been, whether it be an experience of joy or sorrow.

He sees how every jot and tittle of his life, or many lives, in this world or on many worlds have dovetailed, one into the other, and how essential every experience was in order that he might arrive at his present unfoldment exactly on time.

Having made this discovery of his own immortality, he boldly lays hold of his own heart and cries, "Eureka, Eureka."

Knowing that the fountain of life resides within himself, that its waters are pure or defiled according to his own thought he comes into a realization of the fact that he is now a *Free Mason* and no longer bound by the cable tow of necessity.

Being a free worker in the great temple of the Universe, and knowing that every soul is, like himself, of God, and destined for the same goal, he needs take no obligation to regard man as his brother; neither must he be sworn to protect the virtue of woman, because he sees in every woman his own mother, sister or daughter, and in every man a brother.

The discovery of these virtues within himself is not sufficient.

He must incorporate them into his life by living them in his daily contact with humanity and wherever there is a weak strand in his Cable Tow of lives, such as a broken pledge, or an injury done another, his armor will be tested at the weakest part by some temptation great enough to test its breaking power. Should he fail to stand the test he must be re-bound by being re-born, and perhaps live a whole life for the accomplishment of one purpose.

If he stand the test and prove himself worthy, he then becomes a *Free and Accepted Mason* worthy to teach by example rather than by precept.

He becomes a teacher of souls rather than men, and his home a universe, rather than a world. He becomes *The Word*—knowing the truth he speaks truth, and whatsoever he sayeth is true, and whatsoever he doeth, he knows is done for eternity. Realizing this responsibility his wisdom ripens into silence and when he speaks to the multitude he speaks in symbols, knowing they could not comprehend the truth.

Having become a *Free and Accepted Mason* he is entitled to wear the breast-plate, the ancient badge of Free and Accepted Masons, seen upon the King of Clubs.

This badge, when analyzed, reveals the *circle of infinity*, which is bisected by a horizontal line. The upper and lower halves of the sphere would then be symbols of the two great laws of nature: male and female, light and darkness, etc. The horizontal line is intersected by a perpendicular one producing the tau cross. The perpendicular line being a symbol of spirit, the horizontal line that of matter. Taken together the two lines mean the "descent of spirit into matter." The two triangles are symbols of the triune nature of man; also the positive, negative and neutral qualities of matter. When interlaced these two triangles become the six pointed star equal to the six visible signs of the Zodiac, since we can see only one half of this sphere—the other six signs being on the reverse side. Upon the horizontal line will be seen five little spheres—seven spheres in all. These are the seven planets of this solar Universe. Over and above all is a rude resemblance to a bird just taking wing.

This badge when interpreted means that the wearer has traveled the road of infinity; has discovered the light in darkness; has mastered the stars and now controls them by causing matter to obey his will. He is therefore free as a bird to go from planet to planet at will, to build for himself a body out of the elements he finds there, and does not of a necessity have to be born of woman.

He does not make his appearance among mortals except at great intervals, and then only to teach some great lesson or right a wrong.

Such a soul was the Nazarene.

I know of no better way to illustrate the continuity of life than by the accompanying illustration.

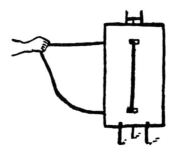

Here is shown a flat surface with two openings and an endless chord reaching from one to the other—a hidden hand draws the chord. The observer sees it enter or come into view at one opening and pass out of sight at the other. The observer knows not the length of the chord behind the surface. So we see life born into the world of matter. We see it pass out through the world of matter, and from that little short span we get a knowledge of the whole.

As the assayer determines the value of the mother lode by the sample, so we may know life and our relation to it by a study of the specimen God gives us from birth to death. Thus it will be seen that the whole object of Masonry, as taught in the various degrees, is told in the Deck of Cards by means of pictures. The story is elaborated and more fully explained by associating the emblems with the various signs of the Zodiac taking care the cards are placed in those signs whose esoteric meaning co-ordinates with the hidden language of the card.

CHAPTER XV.

A Brief Glimpse at the Esoteric Meaning of the Signs of the Zodiac—Aries, the Head, Signifies Strategy, Service and Soul Power; Also the Christ Principle—Cancer, the Breasts, Concentration, Service and Christ—Libra, the Reins, Teach Self Judgment, Service of an Unpleasant Nature—To Lose the Power of One's Kidneys Is to Lose One's Life—Why a Mason Should Protect His Kidneys—Capricorn, the Knees, Symbol of Reflection, Introspection—A Symbol of the Committee of Investigation—The Four Mental Signs, Homes of the Four Knaves, Combine to Make True Birthplaces for the Only Divine Calling, That of the Lawyer.

A still larger degree of unfoldment and a more elaborate explanation is had by considering the functions of that portion of the Grand Man of the Zodiac found in the various Zodiacal signs.

In astrology the sign Aries is always the "rising sign," and in connection with this sign is associated the head of the Archetypal or Grand Man. It is not the purpose of the author to explain here the astrological significance of the Zodiacal signs; such explanation would extend this book beyond the confines of one ordinary volume. To give the reader an insight into the beauties of symbolic readings I will explain the four signs already partly considered in connection with the four Jacks.

ARIES, THE RAM.

If we study the character of the ram we will have revealed to us several strong and prominent features. It fights all its battles with its head, which esoterically means strategy. No greater strategy was ever used than by the Nazarene when answering by symbols the questions put to him. Those symbols have proven the world's greatest mysteries, yet, on the other hand, they were not mysteries at all.

Of the animal kingdom the lamb is regarded as the most docile.

"Be as meek as a lamb" is the divine injunction. "If smitten on one cheek turn the other." "Resist not temptation."

The ram has remarkable genital organs, indicative of great soul power. Christ said "I and my father are one"—showing he was conscious of his unity with God, the soul of the Universe, source of all strength.

The chief characteristic of the ram is that its life seems to be directed toward the growing of a fleece of wool which it annually sheds among the bushes and briars of its native pasture land, thus affording a warm housing for the beasts of the field and the birds of the air to build their nests for their young.

Man, interfering with nature's laws, steps in and forcibly robs the ram of this coat and weaves it into garments and articles of personal adornment. Thus the ram devotes its life to the service of the whole animal world.

"He who would be greatest among you let him be your servant."

In the sign Aries is the head of the Grand Man; this, being the seat of the brain, is also the seat of government of the body, the place of authority. The Ruler of all Rulers is Christ the spiritual King, Son of God. Through the head (mouth) does all food pass into the body, and in the process of mastication it is tasted or tested before its incorporation into the body. Christ said, "I am the door," "I am the way."

By means of the five senses, all of which are centered in the head, we *see* our way through the world of matter, and thus Aries may be said to be the home or window of the soul.

In the east then, where the sign Aries is always rising (the house of the soul) sits the grand master dispensing light, symbolized by the heart in this quarter.

CANCER, THE CRAB.

As has been previously shown, the crab is a symbol of that soul growth when the past and future become merged into the present and the soul realizes that *Now* is eternity, and that time is only an illusion of the mortal mind. It is a symbol of the infinite broken into fragments, but still a unity, as there is one humanity but many units.

In this sign are the breasts of the Grand Man. It is the duty and function of the mammal glands to collect the milk (which of course by its chemical properties represents all portions of the body), bring it to a small point or focus and give of that life substance freely to the suckling infant, who must suck in a proper manner in order to be fed.

Thus the breasts, like the head, teach the lesson of service, and also those other maxims: "Knock and it shall be opened unto you," "Seek and ye shall find." Christ said, "Behold, I stand at the door and knock." Which means that the soul or conscience of every man stands ready and responsive to grant any prayer.

LIBRA, THE SCALES.

Esoterically the scales signify Divine Justice. Being metallic they have no sentiment to express, hence will serve the just and the unjust alike.

From the mystic's standpoint they signify self-weighing, or to quote a Divine injunction, "Judge not that ye be not judged," but they are there in the heavens and they are for use by every soul born into matter. They teach that lesson taught by the Nazarene when, the sinning woman being brought before Him, he asked, "Who accuseth this woman?" and when no one answered He said "Neither do I accuse thee."

The kidneys are said to contain gray matter similar to that in the brain. They are directly connected with the genital organs, hence are said to be the "brains of procreation." Thus, as a symbol, they teach again the work of salvation. The great teacher said he came to save the world from death, and until this law of the soul is understood, until man comes into a full knowledge of his birthright, "rebirth" through this door will be necessary. But the kidneys have another function to perform. They are the great natural magnets of the body, automatically attracting impure gases and foul liquors, and by chemical process producing a purifying effect. Thus the work of the kidneys, in conjunction with the bowels, is to take the offal or excrement from the body for the body's sake.

The same service for humanity was said to have been performed by the Nazarene. He was offered a cup of gall to drink. He drank—and, in verse, in song, we are said to be "washed" by the blood of Jesus.

Into the waters of life all souls are baptized: thus the kidneys become a door to the temple and each and every soul becoming a worker in the grand temple of the Universe comes in through this gateway and takes upon itself the cross of matter, symbolized by the Diamond.

Man's power to reproduce lies in his kidneys. To lose the power of one's kidneys, then, is to lose one's life, to become incompetent. To dissipate this power is to commit moral suicide. To protect man from the dogs of lust and sensuality every Mason is bound to protect the wife, mother, sister and daughter of every other Mason. Having been taught that every man is his brother, this obligation imposes upon a Mason the most virtuous life.

To become a worker in the temple of the Lord the candidate must be perfect and competent. This perfection is symbolized by the two eyes of the Jack of Diamonds and his competency by the quiver of arrows, showing he has power to take life or to refrain and thus give life.

To discover the secret of the kidneys is to discover the fountain of perpetual youth. For the spirit of God moveth upon the face of the waters no more in the beginning of time than at present. Man, being the spoken word of God the following rule of the Ancients will be recognized in its application here:

"No word is efficacious in magic unless it be first quickened by the word of God."

The explanation of the secret is that nature is a great laboratory; that man is the natural magician working out a purpose with such elements as he finds here.

Should he fail to recognize the quickening spirit of God in his own waters of life, he becomes separated from God, or *sexed*, and to become sexed is to become *divided*, and when a soul becomes separated from God it is imperfect.

As man allows his animal, or sexual nature, to dominate he becomes buried, as it were, in the cross of matter, (symbolized by the Diamond), and with that imperfection still clinging to him he strives to solve the problem of death.

CAPRICORN.

The character that represents this sign is so made as to indicate a hinge, which esoterically means "to turn back upon itself." This again means introspection, reflection, contemplation; to hold one's self up as a mirror for examination.

A true Capricorn person is willing to pay all obligations; will even lay down his life in payment of a debt of honor.

The soul who lost his perfection by becoming sexed is symbolized in Capricorn by the Jack of Spades, who has but one eye. Christ himself was imperfect and he said "none is righteous; no, not one."

The knees are the feet of prayer, and as they turn and twist it is a type of the introspection of the soul, a searching for the records of one's life. It typifies the work of the "committee of investigation," who are sent out to ascertain that the applicant is prompted by pure and holy motives and has as a citizen been free from crime and met his least obligations.

Capricorn is the mental sign in the quarter of death (symbolized by the Spade), and when a soul would learn the secrets of this quarter he must be willing to be led by the light of his own soul.

Thus his material eyes are blindfolded; metaphorically he rides Capricornus—the Goat. In other words, the sins of the world are left behind and the Goat or Capricorn becomes the scapegoat.

But the Goat, in symbol, has much to teach us. He is a sure footed animal, symbolizing that man may not guess at the laws of God, but must make sure by testing the spirit to see if it be of God. This does not imply that some other spirit is to be tested or that some departed spirit is to be tested. It means that man must test his own spirit, make sure that his every motive is for good, and when he knows he is walking with God he can, like the Goat, climb to great heights without losing his head or becoming insane as many people do on religious questions.

It was Emerson who said: "High be his heart, faithful his will, clear his sight that he may in good earnest be doctrine, society and law to himself, who has ventured to trust himself for a task-master."

The Goat climbs to great hights, leaps off shelving rocks, striking on its head many feet below and escapes unhurt; in fact, its head is used as a sort of cushion to alight on when necessary to leap from some projecting cliff to the terraces below.

So the soul of man, after reaching great hights of soul power, may find it necessary for its own further development to "leap off" and go down among the lowest depths of humanity and work in the vilest conditions without becoming contaminated by the contact.

Such souls are truly light-bearers.

Again the Goat is a great scavenger; he eats anything and everything, and never seems to get enough.

This is a type of that nature of the soul which prompts it to search in all directions for truth; to investigate all religions, taking from each one that which appeals to him as true and allowing no one creed or ism to claim his entire attention to such extent as to make him uncharitable to his fellow man.

When Christ was asked to give them a sign when they might look for the coming of the Lord He answered and said: "No man knoweth when the Son of Man cometh." This indicates that the secret of God's appearance among men was not entrusted to any one sect or ism.

Those who know God need no salvation.

"The knowledge of evil is not evil but the practice of it."

The twisting and turning principle of Capricorn; the strategy of Aries; the justice of Libra, coupled with the historical character of Cancer; these combine to make the homes of the four Jacks or Knaves true birthplaces for the only Divine calling there is.

With due respect to the profession of the doctor, and a recognition of the sacredness of the "calling" of the priest or preacher, there is but one profession Divine: that one is the law.

The great and prominent characters of the Bible are lawyers, because of their knowledge of God's laws, rather than their preaching and healing powers. Moses never practiced medicine nor preached a sermon, yet he delivered the entire statutes of God on two marble slabs.

When we are sick we ask the doctor to show us his diploma (authority) and inform us of what "pathy" he is; whether he is of the new school or the old. We know we are sick but we are particular as to the means employed to make us well. There are many diseases, a school of cure and a remedy for each.

When the sins of the body weigh heavy and the thread of life is nearly spun and we instinctively turn toward Heaven, we ask the preacher or priest of what creed or ism he is. We know we are sinners, wanting and needing forgiveness, and while the great teacher said there was but one way there seems to be a multitude of light bearers. Each and all claim to have the only light; each would extinguish the others' lights. The sinner stands apart. He is ready to follow a true bearer of the light, but is forced to perish, a mute witness to the struggle between isms, knowing not which to follow, since all claim the same authority for a different form of salvation.

But when we transgress the law and get into trouble we do not ask the lawyer to show his certificate of authority.

We do not ask for his alma mater. We know there is but one law, and that law Divine; its name is Justice. Mortals are wont to symbolize Justice by a female figure holding a pair of balances in the hand, but the sinner and the sinned against look to the lawyer as knowing how to intercede with the court; believing him to be on "familiar" terms with the highest tribunal and able to expound the law of equity between man and man.

Thus the lawyer is, in human affairs, what the Christ is in spiritual affairs and the conscience is in personal matters—a mediator.

Christ never placed the importance upon his healing and preaching that he did upon the law he brought. "He that knoweth the law is become the law."

God's laws are like the public domain—open for settlement to every one. The settler must first make a "discovery" of unoccupied land. He must file his intentions with the public recorder setting forth his purpose. He must then improve the land by cultivation and adornment; by building his home upon it; after a full and complete compliance with all the conditions of the land office, a clear title is given and it is his forever, because he has earned it by becoming one with it.

The body is an expression of the conscience or soul. Spencer says:

"So every spirit as it is most pure,

And hath in it the more of heavenly light,

So it the fairer body doth procure

To habit in, and it more fairly dight

With cheerful grace and amiable sight,

For of the soul the body form doth take,

For soul is form, and doth the body make."

PART VII.

THE MYSTERIOUS WORD
WHICH HAS BEEN MADE SO
MUCH OF IS EXPLAINED BY
THE KABALISTIC CHART
HERE INTRODUCED TO THE
NOTICE OF THE READER—
THIS CHART IS ALMOST SELF-
EXPLANATORY AND YET TO
THE INEXPERIENCED SYMBOL
READER IT REVEALS BUT
LITTLE—IT PROVES HOW
THOROUGHLY KNOWLEDGE
MAY BE BOTH CONCEALED
AND REVEALED BY THE SAME
SYMBOL.

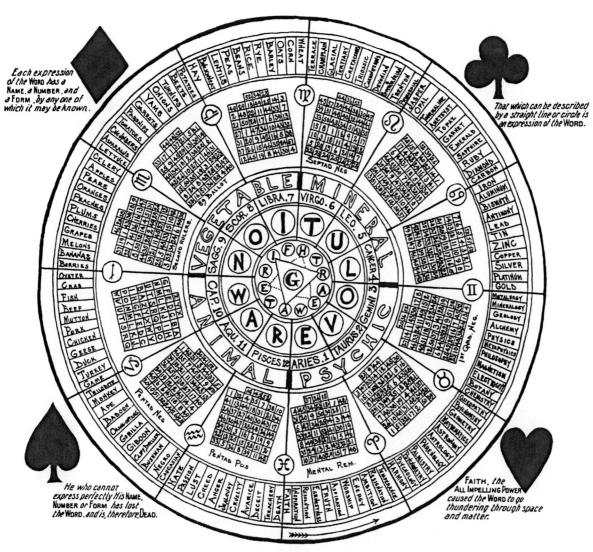

Each expression of the WORD has a NAME, a NUMBER, and a FORM, by any one of which it may be known.

That which can be described by a straight line or circle is an expression of the WORD.

He who cannot express perfectly HIS NAME, NUMBER or FORM has lost the WORD, and is, therefore, DEAD.

FAITH, the ALL IMPELLING POWER caused the WORD to go thundering through space and matter.

CHART No. 2

ARIES - 1

		J♦	K♣	2♣		
4♥	6♠	8♦	10♣	Q♥	A♥	3♠
5♦	7♣	9♥	J♠	K♦	2♦	4♣
6♥	8♠	10♦	Q♣	A♣	3♥	5♠
7♦	9♣	J♥	K♠	2♠	4♦	6♣
8♥	10♠	Q♦	A♦	3♣	5♥	7♠
9♦	J♣	K♥	2♥	4♠	6♦	8♣
10♥	Q♠	A♠	3♦	5♣	7♥	9♠

MENTAL REALM

TAURUS - 2

		10♣	9♥	5♠		
3♥	8♠	7♦	A♣	Q♥	6♠	4♦
2♣	J♥	K♠	10♦	9♣	5♥	3♣
8♥	7♠	A♦	Q♣	6♥	4♠	2♦
J♣	K♥	10♠	9♦	5♣	3♦	8♣
7♥	A♠	Q♦	6♣	4♥	2♠	J♦
K♣	10♥	9♠	5♦	3♠	8♦	7♣
A♥	Q♠	6♦	4♣	2♥	J♠	K♦

GEMINI - 3

			7♣	10♦	K♠	
A♦	A♣	A♥	4♠	4♦	4♣	8♥
7♠	7♦	J♣	J♥	10♠	2♣	2♥
A♠	5♦	5♣	5♥	8♠	8♦	8♣
Q♥	J♠	J♦	3♥	2♠	2♦	6♣
6♥	5♠	9♦	9♣	9♥	Q♠	Q♦
Q♣	3♠	3♦	3♣	7♥	6♠	6♦
10♣	10♥	9♠	K♦	K♣	K♥	4♥

1st QUAD. NEG. *

* Reverse (Right to Left, Descending Order) of Age Spread : 88.
This is due to his incorrect quadration formula, see my comment
in Publisher's Preface.

CANCER - 4

		K♠	Q♠	J♠		
7♥	6♥	5♥	4♥	3♥	2♥	A♥
A♣	K♥	Q♥	J♥	10♥	9♥	8♥
8♣	7♣	6♣	5♣	4♣	3♣	2♣
2♦	A♦	K♣	Q♣	J♣	10♣	9♣
9♦	8♦	7♦	6♦	5♦	4♦	3♦
3♠	2♠	A♠	K♦	Q♦	J♦	10♦
10♠	9♠	8♠	7♠	6♠	5♠	4♠

PURE SPREAD

LEO - 5

		K♠	K♦	K♣		
2♦	2♣	2♥	A♠	A♦	A♣	A♥
4♣	4♥	3♠	3♦	3♣	3♥	2♠
6♥	5♠	5♦	5♣	5♥	4♠	4♦
7♠	7♦	7♣	7♥	6♠	6♦	6♣
9♦	9♣	9♥	8♠	8♦	8♣	8♥
J♣	J♥	10♠	10♦	10♣	10♥	9♠
K♥	Q♠	Q♦	Q♣	Q♥	J♠	J♦

VIRGO - 6

			5♠	10♦	K♠		
6♠	J♦	3♦	7♠	Q♦	4♦	8♠
K♦	5♦	9♠	A♠	6♦	10♠	2♠
7♦	J♠	3♠	8♦	Q♠	4♠	9♦
2♣	8♥	A♥	3♣	9♥	2♥	4♣
10♥	3♥	5♣	J♥	4♥	6♣	Q♥
5♥	7♣	K♥	6♥	8♣	A♣	7♥
9♣	10♣	J♣	Q♣	K♣	A♦	2♦

SEPTAD NEG.

LIBRA - 7

		K♠	8♦	10♣		
A♠	3♦	5♣	10♠	Q♣	A♣	3♥
2♥	9♠	9♣	J♥	5♠	7♦	7♥
8♣	J♠	2♦	4♣	6♥	K♦	K♥
A♦	A♥	8♠	10♦	10♥	4♠	6♦
5♦	7♣	9♥	3♠	3♣	5♥	Q♦
J♦	K♣	2♣	7♠	9♦	J♣	Q♠
Q♥	6♠	6♣	8♥	2♠	4♦	4♥

LIFE SPREAD

SCORPIO - 8

		5♠	9♠	K♠	
7♦	4♣	A♥	J♦	8♣	5♥	2♠
Q♣	9♥	6♠	3♦	K♥	4♦	A♣
10♠	8♦	5♣	2♥	Q♦	9♣	6♥
3♠	K♣	10♥	A♦	J♥	7♠	5♦
2♣	J♠	9♦	6♣	3♥	K♦	10♣
7♥	J♣	8♥	4♠	2♦	Q♥	8♠
6♦	3♣	Q♠	10♦	7♣	4♥	A♠

89 BALLOT *

* I suspect this is the 1888 Presidential election when Benjamin
Harrison (R) was elected President by Electoral College even
though incumbent President Cleveland (D) (b. 3/18/1837 - 5♦)
won the popular vote by a small margin. In 1889, Harrison
(b. 8/20/1833 - 6♣) was inaugurated as 23rd President.

SAGITTARIUS - 9

	7♠	2♦	10♣		

J♦	6♣	A♥	4♠	Q♦	5♣	9♥
9♣	7♥	2♠	10♦	3♣	K♥	8♠
8♥	J♠	6♦	A♣	4♥	Q♠	5♦
5♠	9♦	7♣	2♥	10♠	3♦	K♣
K♦	8♣	J♥	6♠	A♦	4♣	Q♥
Q♣	5♥	9♠	7♦	2♣	10♥	3♠
3♥	K♠	8♦	J♣	6♥	A♠	4♦

SECOND RULERS

CAPRICORN - 10 *

Z	Y	X

G	F	E	D	C	B	A
N	M	L	K	J	I	H
U	T	S	R	Q	P	O
B	A	Z	Y	X	W	V
I	H	G	F	E	D	C
P	O	N	M	L	K	J
W	V	U	T	S	R	Q

ALPHABET

* Note this is exactly opposite **CANCER - 4 : PURE SPREAD**

AQUARIUS - 11

		4♦	2♠	K♠		
A♥	3♠	5♦	3♥	5♠	7♦	5♥
7♠	9♦	7♥	9♠	J♦	9♥	J♠
K♦	6♦	8♣	J♥	8♦	10♣	K♥
10♦	Q♣	2♣	Q♦	A♦	4♣	A♠
3♦	6♣	Q♥	2♥	4♠	A♣	4♥
6♠	3♣	6♥	8♠	5♣	8♥	10♠
7♣	10♥	Q♠	9♣	J♣	K♣	2♦

PENTAD NEG.

PISCES - 12

		A♣	6♠	K♠		
A♥	6♦	4♥	9♦	7♥	Q♦	10♥
2♠	K♥	5♠	5♣	5♦	8♣	8♦
J♣	J♦	A♦	A♠	4♦	4♠	4♣
7♠	7♣	8♠	10♣	9♠	K♣	10♠
3♦	J♠	3♥	3♣	6♥	6♣	9♥
9♣	Q♥	Q♣	2♣	2♦	Q♠	2♥
7♦	5♥	10♦	8♥	K♦	J♥	3♠

PENTAD POS.

CHART NO. 2; OR THE LETTER G.

CHAPTER XVI.

A Kabalistic Chart—Geometry and Masonry Synonymous—
The Tarot—Evolution and War—Faith the Foundation
of All Endeavor—The Heart a Picture of Love—Gold
and God Polar Opposites—Hyram Abif and the Soul
Shown To Be One and the Same.

This chart, like all combinations of mystical hieroglyphs, beggars description.

It is a study, and the student of mystics will find much inspiration resulting from its earnest contemplation.

The numbered squares, the Tarot, have relation to the deck of cards; they are not essential to the chart, nor can they be comprehended by any except those who have been instructed in the esoteric laws symbolized by the cards.

If the reader, however, is desirous of proof that the universe is governed by law, that there is no such thing as chance, that he himself is an expression of the word, that the deck of cards furnishes the key to the secrets of his own soul, let him take a deck of cards and "quadrate" it, first by threes, then by ones.

To quadrate, deal the cards by threes into four piles until only four cards remain. These four last are placed one at a time on the four piles. Now gather them up by placing parcel No. 2 on top of parcel No. 1. Next on top place No. 3, on top of all place No. 4. Now quadrate by dealing one at a time and gathering them up as before. It

will be seen that the first card, or that on top of the pack at the com-
mencement, has gone to the twenty-seventh place, the second card has
gone to the fourteenth place, the third card has gone to first place, and
so on. See Tarot marked "1st Quad. Neg."

This explanation throws but little light on the subject; it does,
however, furnish a key to the earnest student.

There are forty-nine squares (or tiles) in each Tarot presented,
exclusive of the three squares at the top.

There are seven planets in our solar universe. Each planet has
seven squares, three of which are positive, three negative and one
neutral.

The three squares at the top represent the sun, moon and earth.

Consider that our alphabet contains twenty-six letters, that when
these letters are arranged according to their positive and negative
nature in these fifty-two squares, each square, or "tile," will be occupied by a letter, each letter being a symbol of a universal law.

Consider further that this Tarot is only a picture in miniature of
the universal lodge room in which we are all busily engaged carrying out the desires and calculations of the Grand Master. As the
planets move in their orbits forming "conjunctions," "squares," and
"trines," humanity moves too in accordance with these influences,
each individual forming new relations with his fellow man. Each new
move or change of location places him in a different cube or square
of the temple. Each new relation brings with it new obligations, new
duties and their consequent rewards.

Each individual member of the human family has a number and
a name. Each is constantly changing from one "tile" to another or
from one "square" to another, and while his number and name re-

main the same the psychic influences are constantly changing. These forty-nine squares are mathematically the measure of a man; the additional three squares, fifty-two in all, are for the placing of the three great lights of the temple, the three rulers who held the great secret.

To illustrate more fully: A city is divided into blocks or squares, each one of which is numbered on the city plat or map. Each block is again divided into lots, each lot having also a number. Then each lot is divided into feet, and the feet into inches. And each inch has its name and number and exact place in the city.

The Tarots here shown are the minor divisions of the Universal City. The deck of cards, being a mathematical book as well as astronomical, they will when properly mixed, quadrated and spread out, one card on each of the fifty-two squares, reveal to the reader of symbols the exact location in this Universal City of the person so handling them. They will reveal the individual's relation to the rest of the world. They will prophesy the future and lay bare the past.

The letter G so sacred to Masonry has reference to the science of Geometry.

In times gone by Masonry and Geometry were synonymous terms: the method of measuring one's own self in his relation with the rest of the world, by assuming new duties and new obligations, each new obligation becoming a new law to the individual, hence a new Masonic word.

Pythagoras said: "The word is number manifested by form." He also said: "There is the word that expresses, the word that conceals, and the word that signifies."

If the reader can now realize that there is no waste in nature either of matter, of force, of act or of thought, and that every act is eternally registered, he will have some conception of why geometry should be revered as a sacred science.

The stars of heaven are peopled worlds whose thoughts reach unto us upon the wings of light. We are influenced by them, they by us. Geometry teaches the relation of these bodies to each other. We are inhabitants not of this world alone, but of the whole starry universe. To die upon one planet or world means to be born upon another.

A man gives his note for time, his word for eternity. He who prefers the written obligation to the spoken word knows not the law of geometry.

The soul, when conceived, is baptized into the three elements, earth, fire and water. These three elements are symbolized by the triangle, the points of which impinge upon their word equivalents at the points of contact; at the letter "R" in the word earth, "A" in the word water and "I" in the word fire. After nine months of gestation (or temple building by the soul) the diaphragm expands and the fourth element, A. I. R., is added to the first three, and that which was a triangle or circle (inclosure) becomes a square by the addition of this fourth element. At the points of the triangle will be seen the three letters that spell the name of the fourth element.

The soul is a Master Builder because it has caused fire and water (bitter enemies) to love each other and to serve its wish in the building of the human temple.

When the fourth element, "Air," is introduced at the time of birth, the soul functioning from the navel, or solar plexus, may be said to have "raised a dead thing to life," for without the presence of the living soul the four elements composing the body would be dead inanimate matter. Having taken upon itself the cross of matter the soul begins its work of "Evolution" or raising from a lower to a higher degree. It has come from the regions of light or soul. It has been born blindfolded or ignorant. The world of matter is the world of shadow and darkness, therefore the soul cries out constantly for more light, more knowledge, more wisdom.

By referring to the chart it will be noticed that the first *letter* E of the word evolution is in the sign Aries. The second letter (V) is in the sign Taurus and the third letter (O) in the sign Gemini. The entire word occupies nine of the twelve signs of the Zodiac. The other three signs are occupied by the three letters W. A. R.

Evolution must of necessity produce discord or WAR; on the other hand, WAR results in evolution.

Take the first four letters of the word evolution and read them according to one of the Hebrew rules (backward) and we have the word LOVE, the antipode of WAR.

PSYCHIC QUARTER.

It is the psychic nature that loves, and the reader will notice that in the psychic quarter in the first degree of Aries is the word FAITH. In this quarter also is a picture of a flame of fire or a heart. LOVE is the vehicle by which faith travels. How could love be more fittingly symbolized than by making a picture of a heart, and in what manner could life, motion, vibration, be more intelligently suggested than by a candle flame? FAITH then is the all impelling power that caused the word to go thundering through space and matter. Faith is the great prerequisite of all endeavor. Faith followed by *inspiration* brings *resolution* and resolution EARNESTLY kept will reveal the TRUTH.

Truth once discovered brings to the hungry soul that satisfaction which can only be known by the possession of it and results in worship of the provider. Therefore, no sooner does a soul realize its separateness from God than it begins the struggle to return.

Faith being the only power, and love the only medium.

In the psychic quarter are mentioned such principles, arts, sciences and qualities as constitute soul growth.

MINERAL QUARTER.

It is the psychic or soul-world acting upon, in, and through, the mineral kingdom that causes the world of matter.

GOLD is the base of the mineral kingdom; it will crystallize in imitation of all other metals. It is the most universal of all.

Although there are many other simple substances, so called, none is absolutely simple, as gold fluxes with all. Gold may be called the polar opposite of God; it is as natural for man to love and seek gold as to love and seek God.

Metals crystallize, chemicalize and vaporize, thus forming combinations and stratifications producing, after long epochs of time, certain conditions of FORM.

I Kings vii:13-14: "And King Solomon sent and fetched Hiram out of Tyre. He was a widow's son of the tribe of Naphtali, and his father was a man of Tyre, a worker in brass; and he was filled with wisdom and understanding, and cunning to work all works in brass. And he came to King Solomon, and wrought all his work."

Brass being a combination of many metals, it is easy to see

that the Hiram spoken of is the soul. It builds for itself a body out of the metals and crystals of earth. Indeed, without these metals, which have the power to not only take form but hold it, there would be no such thing as body building; no such thing as crystallization; no such thing as growth; development and evolution would be unknown. To work among metals and crystals, causing them to arrange themselves in obedience to will power is a part of the grand plan of evolution.

That which can be described by a straight line or circle is an expression of the WORD.

CHART NO. 2; LETTER G—CONTINUED.

CHAPTER XVII.

GENDER IN VEGETATION—THE WONDERFUL MULTIPLYING POWERS OF CEREALS—THE VEGETABLE KINGDOM EXPRESSES A PART OF THE GRAND WORD—STRUGGLE AND STRIFE NECESSARY TO GROWTH—IN THE ANIMAL WORLD ONLY DOES WAR EXIST—WHEN A BRAIN HAS BEEN EVOLVED AND PREPARED, THEN THE SOUL TAKES POSSESSION—THE HUMAN SOUL NEVER INCARNATED IN ANYTHING LESS THAN THE HUMAN ANIMAL—NAMES AS SYMBOLS—NAMES LIKE THE GRAND WORD IN THREE PARTS.

VEGETABLE QUARTER.

In the journey of evolution *gender* makes its first appearance in the vegetable kingdom. The mineral kingdom merges into the vegetable so unconsciously and with so little effort on Nature's part, that it is difficult to tell just where the two worlds meet.

All the cereals that ripen in the sunshine have great reproductive powers; some scientists claim that because of the wonderful multiplying powers of grains they are such good food products. Of course it is a far cry from the mineral kingdom to wheat; the reader, however, should not think for one moment that in the process of evolution a single gap or missing link exists. Suggestions only are made in the chart.

For the student, however, who will accept a "suggestion" and then contemplate upon it, nature has much in store.

In the vegetable quarter are included the three zodiacal signs Libra, Scorpio and Saggitarius, the former being the sign of the kidneys, or "brains of sexation," and Scorpio, the sign of the sex organs.

Regenerate, rebuild, renew, remake, is the language of these signs.

In the vegetable kingdom, however, there is no throbbing brain, nor pulsating heart to record or express sentiment. Each and every kind reproduces its species without slightest variation for many generations. Left alone the tendency is to retrograde rather than advance, and unless *something* be added from above the species finally dies out. The law for this is that to reproduce is really to divide, and division means subtraction.

The vegetable, having no sentiment to express nor Karmic debts to pay, labors to perfect its form and reproduce its kind in seed and tuber according to its ancestral law. It produces the same seed and the same number of seeds season after season; the same stalk, stem and leaf. The vegetable is not concerned as to what its *name* may be. It puts forth its whole endeavor in perfect imitation of its parent fiber in reproduction of flower, fruit and seed.

NUMBER and FORM is that part of the WORD the vegetable world is called upon to express. How perfectly and faithfully she performs these duties is apparent to the student of nature, when we consider the slight imperfections noticeable; particularly when we consider the seismic disturbances occurring in all parts of the world at all times. Without these atmospheric disturbances no doubt vegetation would be perfect; in form at least. The botanist knows the tree by the fruit, flower, seed or leaf. He reads the history of a plant from a tiny petal.

The metallurgist in his laboratory, from grains of sand, reads backward the history of the world's growth and development. Every crystal brings to him a true record of its life and teaches unerringly that "Each expression of the WORD has a NAME. a NUMBER and a FORM, by any one of which it may be known."

ANIMAL QUARTER.

As we pass from the vegetable quarter to a consideration of the animal quarter, we pass from the word EVOLUTION and are brought face to face with that most cruel of all words, WAR. Evolution results in war, and war results in evolution. Struggle and strife, discord and enmity, are necessary to growth.

Without trimming, pruning, grafting and budding there would be no opportunity for the birth of higher laws and principles into the lower ones.

"Through sorrow man approaches nearest to God."

The passage from the Vegetable world or quarter into the Animal is so narrow as to be almost past discovery; the lowest order of animal life so closely resembles the vegetable that the scientist alone can make the distinction.

In the animal world alone does war exist in the true sense of war. One plant may subsist upon another of a *different species,* but war in its true sense is a contest between elements, factions or forms of like natures and equal powers.

When by the evolutionary process a form sufficiently complex to respond to *Will* and *Sensation* has been produced then animal life begins and war among the species results.

Extermination is the cry from lowest to highest, from the tiniest expression of life to the grandest man.

By means of the brain animals think and reason from cause to effect; by the addition or impinging of one faculty upon another an animal is finally evolved with enough brain power and will force to respond to the human soul and as soon as this animal is prepared the human soul finds incarnation and is thus launched upon the journey of life.

The human animal is the vehicle by or through which the human soul expresses itself. The human soul is never incarnated in anything less than a human body. Any brain or animal less complex would not be sufficient for it.

The "Caucasian" represents the highest type of evolved matter; through his brain does such principles as Hate, Passion, Lust and Greed find expression, directed with the greatest degree of certainty and result. The greater the intelligence the greater the degree of will force.

The greater freedom man gives to his animal nature, the more he allows his evil passions to sway him, indulging in those principles of war in which only the animal can indulge, the sooner he comes to a realization of that great truth:

"That which cannot express perfectly its Name, Number, or Form has lost the WORD and is therefore Dead."

NAME AND NUMBER.

A name is composed of letters and is intended to express a principle. A child is named in honor of some great personage with the hope and belief that it will in some degree express the same virtues as made its namesake great.

Names are in three parts, such as John Henry Smith. Each letter of a name represents a universal law, and all the letters, as a collective whole, represent a larger law.

As an illustration we will suppose the world of matter to be composed of four elements: Fire, Earth, Air and Water, represented by four equal lines. Place within this inclosure a letter, and the impinging points of the letter will indicate the predominating element belonging to that particular letter.

If the reader can now imagine that small square or enclosure so enlarged as to include the Universe, and can imagine that each letter of his name is a vibratory law, reaching from Infinity to Infinity, he will get a faint idea of the power of his own name; if that name be in three parts he will realize the magnitude of the responsibility he assumed when it was bestowed upon him.

By reference to the chart it will be seen that the twenty-six letters of the alphabet are repeated in one of the Tarots. This because the letters have a positive and negative quality, and by repeating they exactly fill the forty-nine squares (the homes of the seven planets) and the three places of Honor assigned to the Sun, Moon and Earth, at the top.

These forty-nine squares are forty-nine geometrical divisfons of the stellar universe. All are numbered and named; and every soul born into the world of matter assumes the name and number of all, but more particularly those names and numbers of squares in which the planets may be at time of birth.

It is the great checkerboard of life.

CHART NO. 2; LETTER G—CONCLUDED.

CHAPTER XVIII.

THE FOUR GREAT EMBLEMS—THE THREE RUFFIANS—NUMBER BELONGS TO THE SOUL REALM AND IS EXPRESSED IN COLOR ONLY—NAME IS CHARACTERISTIC OF THE SPIRIT FORM—OWNED BY THE WORLD OF MATTER—THE ESOTERIC MEANING OF THE TWO VEILS.

THE FOUR GREAT EMBLEMS.

As has been explained in a previous chapter the heart is a picture of a flame of fire and symbolizes light.

Page 65, "Morals and Dogma," Master Degree Lecture: "If, in teaching the great doctrine of the divine nature of the Soul, and in striving to explain its longings after immortality and in proving its superiority over the souls of the animals which have no aspirations Heavenward, the ancients struggled in vain to express the nature of the soul by comparing it to fire and light, it will be well for us to consider whether with all our boasted knowledge we have any better or clearer idea of its nature and whether we have not despairingly taken refuge in having none at all."

It is a ray of light then that goes forth on the wings of faith to find expression in matter. From the soul realm, where all is light and there is no shadow, the soul goes to the other extreme of vibration and finds itself locked in the embrace of crystallized metals.

Instead of functioning upon one plane it now goes to work in regular order and faithfully performing the duty assigned it by the grand Architect builds a natural as well as spiritual body.

These three spheres are symbolized by the clover leaf which shows three complete circles joined together by one stem. It is a symbol of knowledge, showing the first duty of the soul is to acquire a knowledge of its environments. After gaining a knowledge of the material laws, or after passing through "school days," the soul is ready to take up the more serious affairs of life and enter the world of finance, which is symbolized by the Diamond, as he who has diamonds has power on earth. The possession of precious jewels is always most desirable and to him who has wealth much honor is given. It is a proof of soul power to be able to so control men and principles as to acquire wealth. Great enterprises require great minds and soul, or will power, to direct them. All souls are kings; all are subjects. All acquire that which they most desire with all their heart some time, some place, somehow; if not in time then in eternity, as it is the law given by the master of old.

"Whatsoever ye pray for with all your heart, believing, the same shall be added unto you."

If a person thinks evil he need not be surprised if evil visits him.

Epictidus, an ancient philosopher, had this to say: "God gives us that which is our own unhindered and unhampered, and hinders and hampers that which is not our own."

Passing from the Diamond, or wealth quarter, to the quarter of "death," symbolized by the Spade, the soul is met at the door of the temple by three ruffians who would wrest from it the all-powerful Word.

These three ruffians are ever present with every soul from the first breath to the last.

One of them is named Fear; the second Selfishness, the third Ignorance.

FEAR.

Fear of the future impedes the growth and development of the soul. *Fear* that the future wants and necessities of life may not be forthcoming causes man to commit crime against his brother. *Fear* that beyond the grave there may be eternal punishment makes men hypocritical, in the eye of the All-Seeing One a most heinous crime. *Fear* of death makes men, otherwise brave, cowards. *Fear* fills the asylums with insane and robs the soul of its birthright. *Fear* has perched upon the brow of inspiration and stayed the hand that would proclaim to the world some great scientific or religious truth.

Fear has made it possible for self-elected bigots to hold in subjugation nations of people.

Fear brings the sinner to the confessional and takes his last penny for the repose of his soul.

Fear puts the priest in solitude and denies him the joys of love.

Fear causes the mother to swoon away into unconsciousness while her babe plays with the deadly reptile with impunity.

SELFISHNESS.

Selfishness causes men to bear false witness and perjure and blacken the soul for love of gain. A desire to possess for passional gratification causes humanity to murder, abduct and imprison the weak and virtuous.

Selfishness allows the strong to starve the weak. It sits in the lap of the rich and turns the starving poor away with a glad hand.

Selfishness causes brothers and sisters born of the same womb to become bitter enemies.

Selfishness withholds the helping hand in time of need and is often the true test of friendship.

Selfishness rides in the carriage of the aristocrat and the starving multitude begs with outstretched arms for just a little of the golden grain rotting in his granaries.

Selfishness allows his wife and children to make every sacrifice while he revels at the play. Gratification of self when our brother suffers because of it causes the soul to weep with pain and sorrow.

IGNORANCE.

Ignorance of the laws governing our physical bodies causes pain and suffering.

Ignorance of plant life that are compounded into foods produces inharmonious conditions of the body resulting in disease.

Ignorance of planetary law permits man to blunder along in the belief that there are accidents, and when his life is snuffed out by the explosion of a steam boiler or the hand of an assassin or the bullet of an enemy, he awakes in the after life to discover that the universe is governed by fixed and inexorable law, and that while it is true that man is the arbiter of his own destiny, still only *ignorance* will close his perception to this truth.

Ignorance of spiritual laws, rather the laws of spirit, permit some to suffer from obsession and many a soul is born into the world with a deformed body by reason of ignorance on the part of parents regarding the law of spirit.

Ignorance regarding communion between planetary bodies by means of spirit intelligence has dwarfed human progress and kept the door of inspiration closed.

Ignorance of the power of our own will has made poverty, sin, sickness and disease a constant companion.

Ignorance of the power of our own breath, our own mind, our own thought upon our bodies in times of sickness and pain, has robbed life of much pleasure and stunted the growth of the soul.

The lesson of the Spade or rather the Acorn, is to teach that as the acorn has an outer shell, an inner meat and then a germ, so has man an outer body, which like the acorn must die from the parent tree and be buried in the dark recesses of the earth, there to rot, disintegrate and decay; that as the acorn has an inner meat, so has man a spiritual body; that as the acorn has power to send forth its soul in the reproduction of another tree, so man has power to launch forth his soul on the eternal wings of light; that while the acorn is one body there is the dividing line between the outer shell and the inner meat; the division is distinct. So with man there is the three in one: spirit, soul and body.

The only language known in the soul realm is number, which is expressed by Color only.

Name is characteristic of the spirit.

Form is owned by the world of matter.

The circle of the Infinite is divided into four quarters of ninety degrees each. These great divisions are represented in the chart and in each of these quarters there are two divisions or "veils."

These veils are symbols of those other veils dividing the worlds of spirit, soul, and matter, and when we as travelers pass from one world to another, there will be demanded from us by one who sits behind the veil, our name or our number, and "he who cannot express perfectly his Name, Number or Form has lost the Word and is therefore dead," and must be born again, as perfection can be acquired only after many and repeated efforts.

PART VIII.

SOME BIBLE EXPRESSIONS—
MASONIC SYMBOLS AND
OTHER CHARACTERS IN
EVERYDAY USE—THE NINE
DIGITS GIVEN A NEW AND
TRUE EXPLANATION—A SIM-
PLE YET PLAIN BASIS FOR
MAN'S CLAIM TO SONSHIP OF
GOD.

CHAPTER XIX.

IN HIS IMAGE AND LIKENESS

ATOMS AS MIRRORS—HUMANITY UNCONSCIOUS OF HEALTH, BUT AWAKE TO DISEASE—THE HUMAN FAMILY COVERING THE SURFACE OF THE EARTH LIKENED UNTO THE CUTICLE, OR SKIN, OF THE INDIVIDUAL—EACH INDIVIDUAL HUMAN A CENTER CREATIVE, AND THE ENTIRE HUMAN FAMLY THE CIRCUMFERENCE—MASONRY CONCEALS ITS SECRETS FROM ALL EXCEPT THE ADEPTS—USING FALSE EXPLANATIONS AND MISINTERPRETATIONS—TRUTH A DEADLY THING—MAN IN CONSTANT COMMUNION WITH GOD.

Let the reader examine himself and consider the growth of his own body. It had its beginning in the single atom, and by the addition of atom upon atom it grew into parts and members, finally completing the whole body.

The soul being the builder each atom derives its light, life and substance from it; atoms grow into fibers, chords, tendons, muscles and bones; each part owes its life to the soul which seals the atoms with its own personality. In other words, each atom has imprinted upon it the image of the Soul.

If the soul is expressing as "John Smith," each atom composing the body will bear the likeness of John Smith; if these atoms could speak they would say that their name was Smith. All the chords, tendons, and muscles of the body, as collective groups of atoms, would declare their name to be Smith. In like manner the individual bears the likeness of his country or nation—an American, a Russian, an Englishman.

From the standpoint of atoms, Smith would be to them God, though they could not see him nor comprehend him. Such atoms as do the will of Smith and respond to his desires may be said to be "in tune with the Infinite" or be doing God's will (Smith's will).

Smith rejoices in the spontaneous and harmonious response of the members of his body. The soul of Smith is glorified in the beauty, symmetry, strength and health of his body. He is unconscious of health, but at once awakens to disease or pain. He takes no notice of the other members but devotes his entire attention to the sinners, and when they return into harmonious condition or relationship with the soul of Smith (health), it may be said that there is "great rejoicing among the angels for the return of one sinner."

We think not of our bodies except when hunger or disease overtakes us; then we turn our thoughts to it, and especially do we center our thoughts upon those parts that cause the pain. We are willing to neglect, for the time being, the other parts of the body and devote our whole time to the sinner.

God, the Universal Soul, sent His only begotten son into the world to save the sinners; the only instances where Christ really forgave were the harlot and the thief, thus proving the truthfulness of

"Through sorrow God approaches nearest to man;
Through sorrow man approaches nearest to God."

In the cuticle or skin of the human body the bright red arterial blood, full of life and vitality from the heart, changes by some unknown and unseen process into venous blood, dark and void of life.

Around every bone, chord, muscle and fiber, yea, every atom, there is a corresponding cuticle or layer serving the same purpose.

Every member of the body and every atom composing the members is reached by this double set of veins and arteries. Each atom is reached by a double set of nerves also. Because of which, Smith, the soul, can reach all parts of his body, even to the remotest and most obscure portion, and so whatever Smith's will may be, each and every atom *in harmony with him* will know that will and strive to carry it into effect.

We have taken a brief look at the human body, let us now look briefly at the universal body.

Humanity is composed first of the individual corresponding to the atom. The individual merges into the family, the family into the community and the community grows into the tribe and nation, which constitute the world of humanity.

We live on the outside of a big ball called a world. We constitute its skin. This world, though large from our standpoint, is but an atom of matter held in its position by other atoms or worlds, some larger and some smaller, all of which are so close together that it is impossible for one to fly its prescribed path.

"As it is below so it is above."

"The Microcosm is as the Macrocosm."

"Man is made in the image of God."

A good definition of God is given in the following language:

"God is a sphere whose center is everywhere and whose circumference is nowhere."

Each individual atom is the center of its own universe. Atoms grow into molecules and groups, each atom added to the mass requiring a larger intelligence to manifest through that form. Thus the intelligence necessary to manifest as a hand or foot is greater than the intelligence necessary to manifest as a finger or toe.

The intelligence of the hand is included in that of the arm, while the arm is only one of the many members of the body; yet the whole body is only a human atom in the family tree, having its place and sphere of activity. Each human being has its relation to the whole human family, and in its relation to other human atoms is constanly receiving messages from the great Over Soul.

The whole human family, then, becomes the circumference and each individual a center.

Man moves about from place to place at will; he is not *fixed* anywhere. A moving center from which life and light constantly emanate. His mind is confined nowhere, but is everywhere.

In him does the eternal past meet the infinite future. He joins the fathomless depths to the boundless heights.

If we stand in the center of Infinity, not recognizing limitation, we become a mere point like this (.), but when we recognize our material senses we become limited and that limitation can be symbolized by the circle thus, (O)

I quote from "Morals and Dogma," by Pike:

"Masonry, like all the religions, all the mysteries, hermeticism and alchemy, *conceals* its secrets from all except the adepts and sages, and uses false explanations and misinterpretations of its symbols to mislead those who deserve only to be misled, to conceal the truth from them and draw them away from it. A truth is not for those who are unworthy or unable to receive it, or who would pervert it."

"God himself incapacitates men in divers ways and gives to them the power to attain only so much of his laws as is profitable for them to know. *Every age* has had a religion suited to its capacity."

Synesius, a great Kabalist, wrote: "A spirit that loves wisdom and contemplates the truth close at hand is forced to disguise it to induce the multitudes to accept it, as *truth* becomes *deadly* to those who are not strong enough to contemplate it in all its brilliancies."

If we could look at other worlds with eyes as large as this world we would relatively see them as close as the atoms of our own bodies are close together. There is no space between worlds when looked at from the standpoint of a world. They are as close together as it is possible for them to be.

Each world has its central orb or sun from which it derives its light, warmth, and life, the same as each atom in our bodies belongs to some cord, tendon or fiber.

Worlds are formed into groups and constellations which again become *atoms* compared with the whole of creation.

Even the "Milky Way," that grand pathway across the heavens, may be likened unto a small nerve in a small portion of the human body.

Our world is a compact body made up of material from all the other worlds. Our bodies are of the earth and contain the same elements.

The soul of man, being of God and doing God's will, is commissioned to control these elements, not by ravishment or discord, but by peaceful direction of the will.

We have five senses with which we are constantly receiving messages from the great soul of the universe. *These messages are delivered to us in many ways, and we are never at a loss to know what the divine will may be. It is revealed to us through our conscience.* This divine will is revealed in manifold ways; through every person with whom we come into contact, through the reading of books, through conversations, through newspaper reading, or what not. It is the voice of God speaking through that channel, and the soul of God in us responds, either actively or not, according as we are alive to the voice of our conscience.

The soul force that animates a world also animates a universe of worlds. Worlds are peopled, and the *skin of humanity* that covers a world, serves the same purpose to God the cuticle does to the human individual.

Each individual is an expressed thought of the divine will; a message bearer.

Contemplate the greatness of the small and the smallness of the great.

CHAPTER XX.

DIGITS.

Symbolism of the Nine Digits and Cipher—Why Our Mathematical System Includes Only Ten Characters—Why They Are so Formed—A Defense of Lucifer—Why Masons Should Study Mathematics—Gender in Numbers—Every Breath We Breathe Is Numbered, Gendered and Named—A Scientific Explanation of Blessing Food—A Basis for the Science of Astrology—Why Masons Should Study Chemistry, Music and Architecture—The Christian Cross Shown in a New Light—The Double Cross—Sealed by the Stars.

The Mason is admonished to study mathematics. He is not advised to pursue his studies through simple addition and subtraction, there to cease. He is not told to master square root and fractions.

He is not told to go so far and no further. He is simply advised to "study mathematics."

No student would be considered proficient in any study unless he were master of the basic principles and could elucidate the premise of the science, therefore the student of mathematics should know the whys and wherefores of the nine digits and cipher; why there are only ten of them; why formed in the manner they are, and why it is possible to perform such stupendous examples with these ten little characters.

We are wont to handle them and use them with as little regard for their divine worth as a little child would play with a handful of diamonds; never giving a thought to their universal value and the infallible laws they represent.

The first digit or figure one (1) is in reality a diameter of a circle; while it is usually made by drawing a line *perpendicular*, a horizontal or oblique line would be a *perpendicular*, or figure 1, from *some* standpoint, just the same as that expression in Masonry which says "the sun is at high meridian all the time," is true.

The first digit or figure 1 is a symbol of the first great cause, and stands for the Universal Law of God. It is a symbol of Unity as well as a symbol of the trinity. In gender it is both masculine and feminine and adds to those natures the third quality, that of being neuter.

As in the beginning there was one God and all things were included in that one God, so this character stands for and symbolizes that first cause.

In God were both the male and female, so with the straight line or figure one; it has two ends, one positive and one negative, and where these two meet there must be the neuter element. Therefore, this first digit is not only one, but it is two, and it is not only two, but it is three.

In order to find the gender in numbers we must look to Mother Nature, for she can always be relied upon to reveal her most sacred secrets to him who will search in honesty of purpose.

When Mother Nature gives birth to her offspring she does so perfectly, i. e., she divides herself into *two equal parts* without any remainder.

Before birth took place the figure one would represent *all;* at birth the one becomes divided into two parts and the division is perfect; she expunges from herself all her offspring, retaining no fractional part. Not so, however, with Father Nature; when he gives birth to himself he retains a fractional part for gestative purposes. Thus any number that is divisible by two without a remainder is *feminine*, 2, 4, 6, 8, and any number that cannot be divided by two without a fractional part left over is *masculine*, 3, 5, 7, 9.

It is a geometrical axiom that "a circle is made up of straight lines," therefore the cipher in mathematics is in reality a *figure* 1 *drawn out* until the two ends meet. Thus they are both symbols of Infinity.

The cipher is a symbol of feminity because it is an enclosure in which there is no thing. Thus it will be seen that the beginning and ending of our mathematical system is in the Infinite and that the characters we use are symbols of Infinite Law.

In all schools of symbolism, spirit is set forth and symbolized by the perpendicular line, as matter lies recumbent and spirit ascends or descends into it. The figure one then becomes the symbol of spirit which harmonizes with the claim that God is spirit.

2

The second character or digit is feminine, and its form describes the path of the sun through the twelve signs of the Zodiac. As the Tropics of Cancer and Capricorn mark the northern and southern declines of the sun, the path of that orb between these two extremes would be represented by an oblique line.

This is a beautiful symbol of motherhood, since the constant traveling of the sun from one hemisphere to the other produces the seasons, which of course means sexation in nature. The departure of the sun from the Southern Hemisphere means the advent of spring in the Northern Hemisphere, when the husbandman goes forth to sow and the birds and beasts choose their mates.

The sun continues his journey until he reaches his most northern point of declination at which time the Southern Hemisphere is clothed in its wintry garb and may be said to be in the clutches of death, the great life giver having for a time apparently left it alone.

The second character of our mathematical system is thus shown to be distinctly feminine and the first one masculine.

The first breath taken into the body being number 1 is masculine, and our life comes into the body as masculine. The next breath is an *outgoing breath* and is number 2, therefore feminine. Now, if we should take but just those two breaths one would be positive and the other negative; or our life would come in on one and go out on the other and that would be the end of it. But we continue to *inhale* and *exhale*. Therefore the third breath we draw is an incoming breath, and again our life comes in. The No. 3 is not divisible by 2 without a remainder, therefore the third breath is masculine. Again our life goes out on the fourth breath, which is again feminine. Thus it will be seen that each breath we draw is numbered and named according to the gender of it; we also see that every incoming breath is masculine and every outgoing breath feminine. We live in the father and die in the mother.

By a little observation the reader will see that food and nourishment of every kind is taken into the body on the incoming breath. If one takes a drink of water he holds his breath while so doing. All foods are passed into the mouth on a suspended or inhaled breath. Thus does the soul bless every particle of food and nourishment entering into the "temple" with the blessing or breath of life. Having extracted from that food the life sustaining properties needed the waste matter is expelled from the body on the outgoing or death breath. Thus when one expectorates, or sneezes, or vomits, or coughs, it is on the outgoing breath. All excrement from the bowels and bladder is forced into the world on the death or suspended breath. On the outgoing breath of the mother are all children born. As soon as the babe is freed from the mother its diaphragm expands, producing a vacuum at the solar plexus, and the first or No. 1 breath is taken by inhalation. Thus does nature complete the everlasting circuit. As the life escapes the mother it is taken up by the child.

The outgoing breath is then the death breath because the life goes out on that breath; the incoming breath is the breath of life because the life comes in on that breath.

At the time of the first breath the sun, moon and earth and all the planets of this solar universe are in certain *Geometrical* relations to each other within the circuit of Neptune's orbit, and as these monster magnets teeming with life rush through the twelve great divisions of the sun's Zodiac, forming combinations of electric and magnetic forces, we breathe into our bodies with that first breath the blessing of each of those planetary Gods, according to *their place* in the Grand Archetypal Man.

Thus man is born a natural chemist, mixing, blending, harmonizing the chemical properties of the planets; therefore a Mason should study chemistry.

Man is born a natural musician for the reason that each of these planets is the source of a note or vibration in music, therefore, study music, learn its source and become attuned with the dominant chord of one's own soul.

These planets change their relative positions with the rapidity of thought and each change of position means a change of chemicalization in the breathing, pulsating body; therefore man is advised to study architecture in all its branches in order that he may square himself geometrically with the law and order of the universal temple.

To be able to square one's self is to be able to determine whether his acts are in response to the good or evil influence of the planetary Gods. One does not need the advice of a fortune teller, astrologer, palmist, or card reader, to advise him as to his duty, for man has within him an unerring and infallible guide; a guide that never sleeps, is never off duty, and never asks for reward. A recognition of this guide guarantees success, happiness, health and finally a freeing from this earth's attractive nature.   This guide is born with every one.   Its name is *truth* expressed as *conscience.*

To listen to one's conscience is to hear the voice of Christ; to reject the conscience is to kill the widow's son.

The figure 2, then, is a symbol of Universal life and Universal death.

Its form is made of two horizontal lines connected by an oblique line indicating the union of spirit and matter.

The third digit is masculine, and serves as a connecting link between the second and fourth digits, thus performing the duties of a mediator or Christ principle.

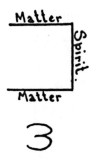

The form of the character is an open square and if we label the two horizontal lines matter the third line will be a true type of the Christ principle (mediator) as it connects the two extremes.

Again by adding the first digit, or No. 1, to the second, the third is produced.   It, then, is the result of all that has gone before it plus its own self.   It represents that great neuter element existing throughout the infinite.

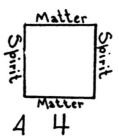

The fourth digit is made by the joining of two perpendicular lines to two horizontal ones, thus making a complete square, the two perpendicular lines being called spirit, the two horizontal ones matter.

It will be seen that after leaving the second digit each succeeding character is a repetition of the preceding one with an additional line added, each line being a symbol of a universal law.

The figure 4 then is simply a picture of an enclosure, a womb, and this enclosure is composed of the four elements Fire, Earth, Air and Water.

The fourth digit is feminine.

By the addition of one more line or principle the enclosure becomes opened, or dead matter is raised to life on the "five points of contact."

Starting with the first digit and calling it "spirit," the second "matter," the third "spirit," and the fourth "matter," the fifth one is charged with the supreme task of raising to a higher level those natural warring elements, Fire vs. Water; Earth vs. Air. When the work is accomplished one side of the cube opens up and one of the perpendicular lines points upward and becomes joined to another horizontal line above, thus picturing the "raising" process from a lower to a higher. This can only be done by a *master* of those elements.

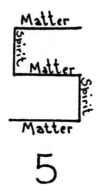

5

The form of the digit is like the letter "S" except the corners are not rounded as in the letter "S."

Five is a masculine number and, as shown, the work assigned to it is that of resurrection, or the life-giving principle.

Within the enclosure represented by the four universal *ones*, the fifth universal *one* takes his place and in due time breaks the seal of death and walks forth free. Thus the fifth digit is a symbol of resurrection, and when applied to human affairs means that those who bear this number are called upon to transmute from a lower to a higher degree their own moral nature.

The soul when born into matter in the midst of these four warring elements is often symbolized by the cube with a dot in the center, the cube representing the elements and the dot the soul or builder.

As the soul controls those contending forces it reaches out in all directions and makes the contact on the four sides or corners of the cube. These four points of contact, plus itself, making five, are set forth as a symbol in following cut.

It will be seen that as the center of this figure is raised or lifted up it describes a perfect pyramid.

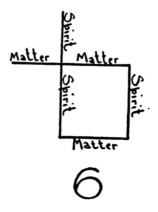

The raising and transmuting process accomplished by the male principle, as set forth in the figure 5, is still further carried on in the next digit, or figure 6. This digit is formed by the addition of both spirit and matter to the four warring elements. In the first resurrection, symbolized by the 5, only spirit, or the masculine principle, was necessary to accomplish the work (York rite in Masonry), but in the second resurrection both male and female are necessary (the Magi).

In the first resurrection only the veil separating the world of matter from the world of spirit was pushed aside, but in the second resurrection the veil between the spirit and soul realm is penetrated and the absolute truth is realized.

The world has a glimpse of this law now; it is being made manifest by a "search after the soul-mate." Those who indulge in this belief labor under the delusion that to find their "soul-mate" would be to end all their earthly woes, whereas, in reality it would be only the beginning of them. Beware of your soul-mate if you would be happy on earth. Let your soul-mate rest in the unseen to be your guide and inspiration. Waste not your substance in vessels of clay, but husband your soul's power (sex power) for use in those greater activities of the soul symbolized by the seventh digit.

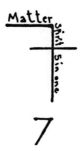

This is again of masculine gender and is a symbol of that law which teaches that after a soul has become rounded out or reunited with itself (discovered its own true self) and by its experience become master over material conditions it is then competent to take charge of other souls and become guide and teacher by the power of will. *An over soul.*

The figure 7 is composed of a horizontal and a perpendicular line, the latter joined at right angles to the former line and extending far below the base line. The long stem is the fifth digit presenting itself as *one,* embracing within itself all the four elements and the spirit of life besides. Thus the two above, as spirit and matter joined in the previous character (6), now reach down and assist in the work of resurrection and transmutation as being carried on by the 5th.

He whose number is 7 will find his path of life strewn with trials and tribulations. To express this law perfectly one must be able to meet defeat with a smile and expect defeat at every turn in the road.

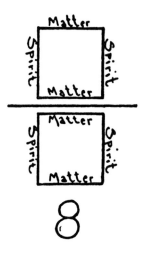

To the seven universal ones we now add another; lo and behold, the result is the double cube or the four elements united above and below the neutral line. This digit represents great soul power and is a symbol of perfect equilibrium, as that which is above is just equal to that which is below. It means that the spiritual and material natures are evenly balanced and harmonized.

Open these two cubes by the process shown in the chapter on

the diamond and it will reveal the double cross so sacred to Masonry and the church.

If the world has so far failed to produce a soul with sufficient strength and wisdom to carry the cross of matter, symbolized by the 4th digit, cube, or cross, what must be the progress made before a soul will be evolved with sufficient strength to pick up the double cross and carry it as symbolized by the figure 8. The figure 8, the double cross, and the double cube, all are symbols of one and the same law

It is a symbol of the law which enables a soul to penetrate into the lowest depths of sin and then vibrate to the highest condition of angelic love. The conception of Milton's "Paradise Lost," Swedenborg's "Heaven and Hell," are illustrations of the soul development possible as symbolized by the figure 8.

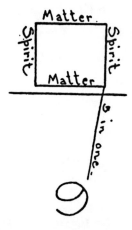

The ninth digit is made by the addition of one more line or law to the preceding figure. Once more the base line serves as a veil be-

tween the upper and lower worlds (so to speak), and the long stem
below the line while only one, is the same *five ones* in one we met at
the fifth step in this spiral stairway, and the four ones above the base
line added to the five ones below give the next masculine principle.

But the raising power, or the Christ principle, is below the four
elements which represent gnomes, vampires and those demons of the
earth conditions. And they of themselves have no desire to rise or be
transmuted. The Christ principle is buried deep in the offal of humanity. This digit represents the fallen angel, as he who has the
number 9 as a birthright learns, like Job, that all is vanity and vexation of soul. He learns that calculations are not to be depended upon
and will even question the correctness of mathematics, so often is he
disappointed in the affairs of life.

Through great sorrow, however, are souls brought nearest to
God; after the swing of the pendulum into the abyss of matter, the
next step is to be united with God in conscious work of salvation, becoming truly a "Lu-cipher" (i. e.: Luce-cipher, luce meaning light and
cipher darkness), which can best be pictured forth by the symbol of the
sun which is a point within a circle.

Having started with the figure 1 which, as has been shown,
is a fraction of a circle, it then stands to reason that back of the one is
the circle (O) or cipher, which of itself signifies nothing or infinity. Thus when the circle of infinity is placed before the 1 it

means No-Thing; placed after the one, it means the Ten Law-making Bodies of this Solar Universe—Sun, Moon and Planets.

In making our digits we round the corners, thus carrying out the divine order to "beautify and adorn" our work. The authority for so doing is found in nature's laws. The reader is referred to the series of cuts and illustrations, in the chapter "Tiled Floor," by aid of which I hope to be able to make myself understood.

The first cut is a representation of the sun sending his rays of light in all directions, but for our purpose we will follow only one ray.

This one ray of energy goes forth in a straight direction and will so continue until it meets an opposing ray exactly like it; then the two rays or forces will be turned at right angles (see cut No. 2), when again they will proceed in straight lines until they again meet opposing forces having the same potency or degree of vibration. Then again they will be turned at right angles (see cut No. 3).

This process of meeting and turning is kept up until the ray is finally turned back upon itself and becomes united with itself, as shown in cut No. 7. This reunion with itself forms a perfect square and might again be called the *Grand Discovery,* or the Squaring of the Circle. If the source of energy were now cut off the forming or completing of this square would be the only result, but the supply being infinite and the stream eternal the corners of these two squares are played upon like a stream of water from a fireman's hose, the square or cube begins to move in a circular direction, increasing in velocity until the corners disappear entirely and that which was *square* becomes *round.*

Thus is centrifugal and centripetal motion established. This result is first obtained and symbolized in the fourth digit and finds expression in the fifth on the five points of contact. Thus is found the authority for the present form of our mathematical characters and the rounding of the corners.

In the figure 8 the law is most beautifully expressed by the two cubes, one above, the other below, the base line; one representing positive, the other negative conditions; turning in opposite directions and joined at the center, as shown by cut No. 8.

By rounding the corners of the cube in the figure 9 thereby producing a circle, and adding thereto the perpendicular line which represents five ones, we have the following result: five below plus four above equal nine.

In the order of creation, so far as our physical bodies are concerned, the active principles of which they are made come first from the sun, earth and moon in the order named (soul, body, spirit). The action or influence of these three is necessary for the beginning of life. If the incarnated soul be strong enough to master the chemical properties of these three, he may be considered a "master builder" and entitled to the *custody of a greater secret* of law which is the law of Mercury.

After being tested and tried by this messenger of the Gods for three months and being found worthy, we are "sealed" by him and then introduced to the beautiful and musical goddess, Venus

for further instructions. Under her tuition we beautify and ornament the temple and bring it nearer completion. Venus, the mother principle, and in mathematics, the figure 5, bear us anew.

Mars,

the warrior, then develops our intellect and causes an awakening of the mental faculties, he being the sixth tutor in this universal school.

Jove or Jupiter

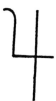

represented in mythology as Atlas carrying the world on his shoulders, teaches us the laws of strength and power and fortitude that
we may be able to meet the evil influences of Saturn or Satan, to
whose spiritualizing influences he turns us over in our twenty-ninth
year.

Jupiter's number is 7. He is considered the great balance wheel
of the heavens and governs the business affairs of men.

Saturn

with his rings and moons is the eighth number of this universal
household; as has been shown, he who can carry the cross of Saturn
has "carte blanche" to enter the worlds of spirit and matter.

Uranus or Herschel is the representative of law, symbolized by
the number 9. This planet is said to be a patron of the agriculturist,

the delver in the ground, and a friend to the poor, for he causes by
death (ere the eighty-fourth year) a redistribution of the treasures of
the earth: the natural term of life is less than a Uranian year and the
wealth of the rich becomes divided among the poor.

This planet is also said to revolve on its axis centripetally
(toward the center); thus its influence is to turn back into the caldron
of material forces those souls who have not yet made sufficient
progress to venture beyond the confines of this particular solar
universe.

Once past Uranus the traveling soul is launched upon the great
ocean of worlds, suns and systems of suns by our outer planetary
sentinel, Neptune, representative of the tenth law of creation, whose
three-pronged scepter has ever proclaimed him God of Water and
ruler of journeys and voyages.

Thus do the ten digits stand for and symbolize the ten great
magnetic bodies of this universe, the cipher all beyond and outside our
solar system; the planets or stars of heaven are numberless, so also are
the powers and possibilities of numbers limitless.

The ten digits and the ten spot cards are symbols of the same
laws; to the reader of symbols one is as sacred as the other.

The astronomical symbols or characters representing the planets
are made of circles and crosses, thus indicating the sacredness of
the science of astronomy and astrology.

CHAPTER XXI.

THE MASONIC TILED FLOOR.

The Surface of the Earth the Tiled Floor of the Universal Lodge—Each Atom of Matter a White or a Black Square —How the Tiled Floor Teaches the Lesson of Evolution —Suns Like Individuals, Have Their Polar Opposites— How the Square Becomes a Circle—A Mason's Every Thought Is on the Square—Man a Creator of Life Within Himself—The Nature and Longevity of All Life Dependent Upon the Size of the Square Made by the Creating Soul, Whether It Be a Square of the Universe or Only a Man's Body—Five Points of Contact Illustrated by the Rose Croix.

As we walk the surface of the earth we must not forget that it is the great floor of the universal lodge of which the blue canopy of heaven is the royal arch. Each atom of matter is either positive or negative, therefore it is by reason of this characteristic of matter that growth and decay is possible. One atom attracts another, these two a third, and these three a fourth. Thus growth is produced. By reversing this process decay is the result.

Fire and water are bitter enemies; earth and air are also polar opposites. Consequently, when the Soul—which is the life of a thing —has left it, these elements return to their own place. This process is called disintegration, decay, death. If, then, each negative atom be symbolized by a black square (black meaning feminine), and each positive atom being symbolized by a light or white square (white meaning masculine), one can readily understand what is meant by the tiled floor.

As we walk the ground we are constantly reminded of the two great forces in nature, male and female. These two forces being coeternal and coexistent, thus the surface of the earth from horizon to horizon is the great tiled floor of the universal lodge of which each human soul is a member.

What a beautiful and sublime lesson the candidate should learn from this. No lodge is competent to transact business until the floor is properly tiled. This is only symbolical language setting forth the fact that every soul when born into matter must recognize these two contending forces, male and female, life and death.

It also teaches the lesson of evolution and in a mute language tells of the eons and eons reaching from that remote period of the world's history when it was in a nebulous condition, to that epoch when by chemical processes the original elements had formed a crust sufficiently nutritious in vegetable matter to support the vegetable world.

It tells in symbolic language the growth of the mineral and vegetable kingdom into the animal, and how the lowest order of the animal world finally developed into the human animal, which was the final preparation for the birth of the human soul.

The black and white squares tell of the positive and negative atoms which first formed into crystals (salt), thus producing a foundation upon which the world of matter is builded.

The great universal lodge is not prepared for the advent of the human soul until crystallization has done its perfect work through evolutionary processes; it cannot be said to be properly tiled until this work is accomplished.

The following series of illustrations aptly sets forth the process by which the grand tiler of the universal temple performs that duty.

In cut No. 1 of the series is shown the sun or soul of the universe. From it a ray of energy or force goes forth. It will proceed in a straight direction until it meets an opposing force *exactly like itself.*

A force having a greater or less degree of vibration would not stop it; might turn or bend it, but to cause it to be divided, separated and turned back, the opposing forces must be coequal.

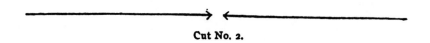

Cut No. 2.

If two streams of water issuing from two pipes be of the same dimension and have the same power, each will be turned back upon itself. Neither one overcomes the other.

Suns, like individuals, have their polar opposites; every ray of light emanating from a sun is sooner or later turned back upon itself by a ray exactly like it, issuing from another sun, and this dividing or turning of the two forces is shown by cut No. 3.

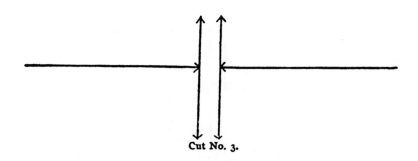

Cut No. 3.

Again these two forces will proceed in straight lines indefinitely until met by other opposing forces exactly similar.

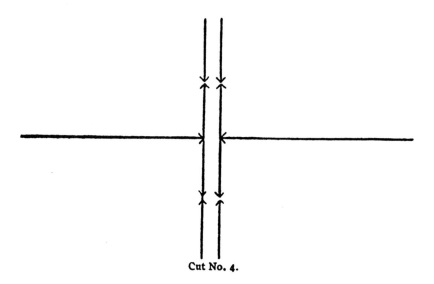

Cut No. 4.

Again they are turned and proceed in a direction at right angles with their former course.

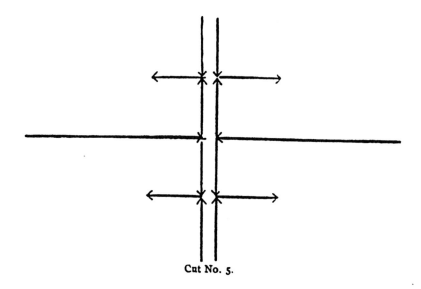

Cut No. 5.

Proceeding further upon their journey these forces again meet their exact opposites as shown in figure 6.

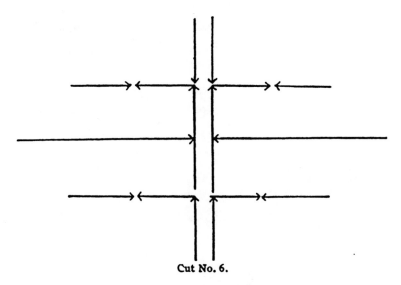

Cut No. 6.

This force is still free to travel in a straight direction and will do so until it finally returns to its ownself, and the *instant* the union is made a *square* is the result as is shown in cut No. 7.

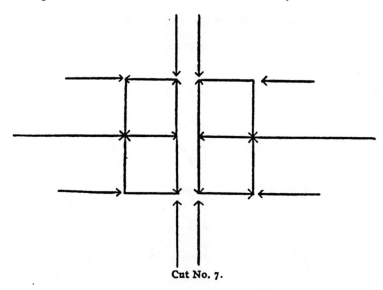

Cut No. 7.

The source of this energy being infinite, the corners of the square are played upon, so to speak, and thus is circular motion set up, life is

generated, and that which was square becomes round, the upper
square revolving in an opposite direction to the lower one as is shown
in cut No. 8.

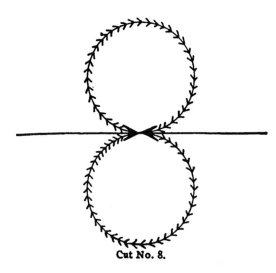

Cut No. 8.

The nature of the life so generated, the size of the square and
circle, are dependent upon the source of the generative force which
includes the square of the universe, and man's mind only operates
within the circle and square of the world.

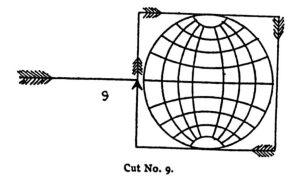

Cut No. 9.

All created life is the result of this law, and within man's own
body there are forms of life that conceive, give birth, live and die of

old age in a few moments of time, the result of his own energy or thought meeting opposing energy or thought within his own circle and square, the limitations of which are confined within the cuticle of his own body. Thus man's own organization becomes a battle ground for the supremacy of life and death.

In the great circle of the earth man himself is a rushing stream of energy, crushing some, being turned, twisted and bent by others, but sooner or later meeting his polar opposite; it is then he finally becomes a conscious creator causing those elements that heretofore subjugated him to obey his will.

In cut No. 7 is shown the ray of light as having returned to its source and become united with itself. Should the supply be cut off now we would have only a square but, the source of energy being eternal, the square is fed and played upon and given a circular motion; in other words the square corners become rounded, producing centrifugal motion and causing a vacuum or place where *nothing* is and where no "thing" is (that which has form and parts), there msut be light or life because light implies motion, consequently life.

Intelligent life is master over the dead materials of earth (symbolized by the square); thus the dead thing is raised on the five points of contact or fellowship, for, be it remembered, each line, dot, or circle is a symbol of a universal law, and in the square or cube we have the four sides plus the "one" in the center making five. This one in the center uniting itself with the other four is beautifully symbolized in the Maltese Cross.

which shows how the living soul in the midst of the dead elements raises to a living stature the four warring elements, fire, earth, air and water. The earth being feminine, she it is must conceive, but she can conceive only in elements of which she is composed; these are the four universal ones. They are constantly warring with each other, as water against fire.

The soul or light or sun of God is baptized at the time of conception into the waters of gestation where it finds but three elements with which to work, viz.: *Fire (manifested by the heat of the body), Earth (manifested by the bones, or crystallization, water, liquids of the body).

The Soul, being a builder or Mason, must take the raw materials and without sound of any metal tool build a temple (body) from these three elements alone; hence, in Masonry, no Mason is a Master until he has taken three degrees, each degree being a symbol of the overcoming of the universal elements. Each degree represents a struggle or strife for victory.

At time of birth of the physical, the diaphragm expands, pro-

---

*These three elements are repeated four times by the four triangles composing the cross.

ducing a vacuum at the solar plexus. The "air" rushes in through the nostrils and mouth; the babe stretches its little legs, throws out its arms, cries, and thus, *to the three existing elements a fourth is now added*. Thus, the Soul (the Master) who has overcome the three degrees, or elements, working in darkness during the nine months of gestation, now takes up the living cross, symbolized by the perpendicular body and the outstretched arms (✝), and in reality does raise the "dead thing" to life; a fact which could not be accomplished excepting by the five points of contact. The soul functions at the solar plexus or navel, it being at the central point where the four halves of the body (upper half, lower half, right half, left half) unite. Therefore none but a master builder can raise a dead thing to life.

CHAPTER XXII.

MAN UNIVERSAL.

MAN'S MIND IS EVERYWHERE—POSSIBLE FOR CLAIRVOYANTS TO SEE
THE SAME PERSON IN DIFFERENT PLACES AT THE SAME TIME—
THE READER IS INVITED TO TRY A SIMPLE EXPERIMENT AND
PROVE THE UNIVERSALITY OF HIS OWN MIND—MENTAL ACRO-
BATICS—MEMORY A FACULTY OF THE MIND, NOT OF THE BRAIN
—PROPHECY THE ART OF READING THE MIND—MATTER A
VEHICLE OF MIND—ALL OUR THOUGHTS, ACTS AND DEEDS,
NOW AND FOREVER, RECORDED IN THE ATOMIC WORLD—A STU-
PENDOUS THOUGHT—A GLIMPSE AT OUR OWN FUTURE.

How and why man is universal is proven by those illustrations
used in setting forth the law symbolized in the tiled floor. Spirit is
the thought form of the body; as the soul or light, starting forth from
its source, continues until it meets an opposing ray or force having
exactly the same number of vibrations, so of spirit or thought form;
when turned from its course it, too, proceeds in a straight line until
turned again by meeting an opposing force exactly like itself, and so
on, until reunited with itself, thus forming a mind circle. So man's
mind extends or IS in all parts of the world at the same time; because
of this fact it is possible for him to THINK or BE IN THOUGHT
in any part of the world or in many places of the world simultane-
ously. Were it not true that man's mind extends to all parts of the
earth he could not think beyond his own body; *being true*, however.
it is possible for the same mind or person (or perhaps more correctly

speaking the same *intelligence*) to be seen in different localities by clairvoyants and trance-mediums.

The reader is here invited to test the truth of this statement by the following simple experiment:

Seat yourself in the center of a room, close the eyes; imagine you see yourself fully dressed just as you are, standing against the wall in front of you; shut out of your mind everything but yourself; simply picture yourself in thought as though looking into a mirror. Having attained sufficient proficiency to picture yourself as standing in front of you, you next picture yourself as standing on the right side of the room, thus holding two images in the mind at once. You then add a third image of yourself to the two previous ones, seeing yourself on the left side of the room, now you are seeing yourself in three different places at once. As soon as the mind, or will, becomes accustomed to this exercise. you can add a fourth figure by seeing yourself standing against the wall in the rear of the room. This may seem an impossibility, but I assure you is an easy task and quite enjoyable.

Having succeeded in letting go of yourself sufficiently to see yourself at the four sides of the room as directed, try to fill in the spaces between the four personages or images by multiplying yourself: imagine yourself multiplied sufficiently to fill the spaces, thus forming a ring. The ring,. of course, will be an endless chain made up of images of yourself. Now enlarge the ring so as to include the city or town in which you live, by seeing yourself multiplied enough to form a circle entirely compassing the city or locality. Enlarge this circle again by taking in the county or state, or the nation; then enlarge again by taking in the whole earth. Now retrace your steps by letting go, first the earth, then the nation, then your city or town, back to the room; then let go the images forming the ring, let go the image back of you, now the one on the left, now on the right, now the last. By means of this exercise the will gets a splendid treatment. It is not a difficult feat after a little practice.

Reverse this process and visit your own interior self. Picture yourself about an inch long standing on the inside of your own skull in the front part of the head. After the first image is established add the others as before directed. Your own brain will then be spread out before you. You will see both its hemispheres, its folds and convolutions. If you talk to it, each atom will take on a form and look exactly like yourself. You will be surprised at the information one is able to acquire from a conversation with one's own brain.

If your curiosity should lead you further and you wish to visit other portions of the body you can do so by reducing these four figures of yourself to the first one. Now boldly follow the nerves from the brain to any portion of the body you may wish to visit. If your liver is out of order you may pay it a personal visit, talk to it, as though it were a personality (as indeed it is); many times the response is marvelous. Hypnotists will find in this a great aid in the cure of diseases in their subjects.

That the mind or spirit is not confined to the brain is susceptible of proof in various ways.

The brain of to-day is not the same as that of youth, yet the events of youth are readily recalled to-day. A person who has ever been in New York City, Chicago and San Francisco can stand at Kansas City and readily recall the scenes and incidents of his visit to the other cities; in fact he can, in thought, live them all over again.

Those cities do not come to him, he does not go to them; years may have elapsed since his visit and of course his brain has changed many times. Therefore "if his mind did not extend" to those points he could not imagine himself there.

If the mind did not hark back to the days of youth we could not recall the events of youth. If this be true and our minds do extend back, may not it also be true that our minds extend into the future? This, of course, offers a solution of the law of prophecy, whether the prophet be a clairvoyant, palmist, phrenologist or astrologer; all these various sciences being means of *measuring the mind*.

Prof. Oliver Lodge launches the following theory: "There are those who have surmised that matter is, after all, only the weapon and vehicle of mind. The way it interprets itself in our consciousness through the sense of the organs gives no clue to its nature. A motion and alteration of the configuration of the molecules of our brain are believed to accompany every act of thought.

"It will be, at any rate, a suggestive analogy if a material process of an essentially similar sort is found to be occurring throughout what we know as the inorganic world—the world of dead matter —and we should begin to ask, does all this motion correspond to some universal thought or mental activity likewise?"

I quote from "Morals and Dogma," by Pike:

"Even the pulsations of the air once set in motion by the human voice cease not to exist with the sounds to which they gave rise. Their quickly attenuated force soon becomes inaudible to human ears. But the waves of air thus raised perambulate the surface of earth and ocean and in less than twenty hours every atom of the atmosphere takes up the altered movement; due to that infinitesimal portion of primitive motion which has been conveyed to it through countless channels, and which must continue to influence its path throughout its future existence.

"The air is one vast library on whose pages are forever written all that man has ever said or even whispered.

"There in their mutable but unerring characters, mixed with the earliest as well as the latest signs of mortality, stand forever recorded, vows unredeemed, promises unfulfilled; perpetuity in the movement of each particle, all in unison, the testimony of man's changeful will.

"God reads that book through; we cannot. *So earth, air and ocean are eternal witnesses of the acts that we have done.*

"No motion impressed by natural causes or by human agency is ever obliterated.

"Every criminal is by the laws of the Almighty irrevocably chained to the testimony of his crime, for every atom of his mortal frame through whatever changes its particles may migrate, will still retain, adhering to it through every combination, some movement derived from that very muscular effort by which the crime itself was perpetrated.

"What if our faculties should be so enhanced in a future life as to enable us to perceive and trace the ineffaceable consequences of our idle words and evil deeds and render our remorse and grief as eternal as those consequences themselves?

"No more fearful punishment to a superior intelligence can be conceived than to see still in action, with the consciousness that it must continue in action forever, a cause or wrong put in motion by itself ages before."

And then the immortal Emerson says:

"There is no great, no small,
To the soul that maketh all;
And where it cometh all things are,
And it cometh everywhere."

CHAPTER XXIII.

THE LION'S GRIP.

MISINTERPRETATION BY MASONS OF THEIR SYMBOLS—THE LION'S
GRIP SAID TO BE A RELIC OF SUN WORSHIP—THE THREE
RUFFIANS CLAIMED TO BE THE THREE WINTER MONTHS—A
WIDE GUESS AT THE CRUX ANSATA—ITS TRUE MEANING A
UNION OF THE SEXES—A MEMENTO OF THE PHALLIC RELIGION
HANDED DOWN TO US—THE CRUX ANSATA AND THE FIGURE
SIX SYMBOLS OF THE SAME LAW—WHY WOMAN CANNOT BE
A MASON—THE ENTIRE LESSON OF MASONRY TAUGHT IN THE
THREE FIRST DEGREES, ENTERED APPRENTICE, FELLOWCRAFT
AND MASTER.

*Crux Ansata and the Cross of Eternal Life, All Symbolic of
the Soul, the Union of the Male and Female Principle.*

The true meaning of the lion's grip is so deeply buried in
the myths, the legends and the past history of Masonry that the most

learned Masonic writers of to-day fail to reveal its true significance.

I wish to quote from a work by Robert Hewitt Brown, 32°, entitled "Stellar Theology and Masonic Astronomy." The work shows deep thought and extensive research. Mr. Brown says:

"On the 21st of June when the sun arrives at the summer solstice, the constellation Leo, being but 30° in advance of the sun, appears to be leading the way and to aid by his powerful paw in lifting the sun up to the summit of the Zodiacal arch. April and May are therefore said to fail in their attempts to raise the sun; June alone succeeds by the aid of Leo. When at a more remote period the summer solstice was in Leo and the sun actually entered the stars of that constellation at the time of his exaltation, the connection was more intimate and the allegory still more perfect.

"This visible connection between the constellation Leo and the return of the sun to his place of power and glory at the summit of the arch of heaven was the principal reason why that constellation was held in such high esteem and reverence by the ancients."

The astrologers distinguished Leo as the "sole house of the sun" and taught that the world was created when the sun was in that sign. Quoting from Dr. Oliver, Mr. Brown says, "The Lion was adored in the East and the West by the Egyptians and the Mexicans.

"The chief Druid of Britain was styled a Lyon. The national banner of the ancient Persians bore the device of the sun in Leo. A lion couchant with the sun rising at his back was sculptured on their palaces.

"Dr. Oliver seems, however, to have entirely overlooked the true reason for this widespread adoration of the lion.

"The ancient device of the Persians is an astronomical allegory.

"It might well be adopted as an astro-masonic emblem by us. After the sun leaves Leo the days begin to grow unequivocally shorter as the sun declines toward the autumnal equinox to be again slain by the *three* autumn months, lie dead through the *three* winter ones and be raised again by the *three* vernal ones. Each year the great tragedy is repeated and the glorious resurrection takes place. Thus as long as this allegory is remembered the leading truths of astronomy will be perpetuated and the sublime doctrine of the immortal nature of man and other great moral lessons they are thus made to teach will be illustrated and preserved."

Further on the same author speaking of the "Crux Ansata" or the cross of eternal life says: "The specific ancient Egyptian *emblem of eternal life* does not appear to have been adopted in its complete form by other nations, that is, as a letter. Its form was abbreviated, although its symbolical meaning was retained to some extent.

"The Egyptian symbol of eternal life in its unabridged form, as will be seen, is nothing more than the 'tau cross' surmounted by a circle, sometimes made somewhat oval in shape. The entire hieroglyphic was probably originally the picture of the head and horns of a bull, *surmounted by the orb of the sun,* thus expressing in a still more direct and specific manner the sun in Taurus.

"It was thus they were accustomed to represent *Apis.* This symbol from its constant use at first as a sacred emblem, and finally as a letter or hieroglyphic, would naturally assume more and more of an arbitrary form.

"The face and horns of the bull would gradually take shape of a cross as before described and the orb of the sun which surmounted it, lose somewhat its perfect circular form.

"If this conjecture be correct it fully explains why this peculiar symbol denoted among the Egyptians eternal life.

"This Egyptian emblem was subsequently named the *Crux Ansata,* or 'cross with a handle,' because it was thought the circle was nothing more than a handle for the purpose of carrying the cross. It is, in fact, often represented as being so carved on the sculptures, but quite as frequently otherwise. The following cut, reproduction of ancient symbols, shows the 'sign of life' held by the lower end in the hand of the double goddess of truth and justice.

"The idea advanced by some that it is a key derives little or no support from the monuments; besides this, the Egyptian form of a key was entirely different.

"The Crux Ansata was adopted by the early Christians of the East as an appropriate symbol of their faith. The old inscriptions of the Christians at the great Oasis are headed by this symbol and it is also found in some of their monuments at Rome.

"Among the ancients the cross in this form (−|−) was also considered a sacred emblem, pointing, as it does, to the four quarters of the heavens and embracing both the celestial and terrestial hemispheres.

"It was thus a symbol of the universe and expression of the perpetual life and endless duration of nature.

"The Rosicrucians also taught that this form of the cross was the symbol of light because it contained in its formation the ancient Roman letters L V X (*lux*) the Latin word for *light*. Whether this beautiful conceit was invented by them or derived from ancient sources is unknown.

"The tau cross is, as has been shown, an ancient symbol of Egypt, denoting salvation and eternal life.

"The triple tau, being a combination of the tau cross three times repeated, teaches us that we have an immortal part within us that shall survive the grave and which shall never, *never*, NEVER die."

To show how near(?) Masonry interprets her own symbol I
quote again from Mr. Brown his explanation of the above hieroglyphic taken from ancient Egyptian ruins. To the reader of symbols
it is an almost priceless picture:

"The form that lies dead before the altar is that of Osiris, the
personified Sun God, whom the candidate represents in the drama of
initiation lying dead at the winter solstice.   The cross upon his
breast refers to the great celestial cross or intersection of the celestial
equator by the ecliptic.   The figure of the lion grasping the constellation Leo and the summer solstice, at which point the sun is raised
to life and glory, as has been explained in the allegory of the resurrection of the sun, denotes that the candidate is about to be raised from
a symbolical death to life and power by the grip of the lion's paw.
This is made clearly manifest from the fact that the lion holds in his
other paw the ancient Egyptian symbol of eternal life or the *Crux
Ansata.*   The tablet at the feet of the candidate has inscribed upon
it in hieroglyphics the sacred names of *Amon* and of *Mut,* the life of
Amon Ra and probably that of the royal candidate.

"The figure erect at the altar is that of the grand hierophant attired as Isis, with the vacant throne upon her head, emblematic of the departed sun god.

"She has her hand raised in an attitude of command, her arm forming a right angle. Her eyes are fixed upon the emblematic lion as she gives the command that the candidate be raised from death and darkness to light and life.

"There is no doubt but that the whole device is a symbolical picture of the initiation of some important person into the mysteries, not of Osiris but of Isis, who, represented by the Grand Hierophant, stands behind the altar giving the command to raise from death Osiris who lies before it.

"This ancient Egyptian drawing is a strong and startling testimony of the entire correctness of the astronomical solution of the legend of Osiris and that of Hiram. It is, indeed, almost impossible to make an emblematic drawing which would be in more perfect harmony with it."

Mr. Brown arrives at a true solution of the symbol, (Crux Ansata) in so far as it is a symbol of eternal life, but he fails to see in the circle and cross a picture of the sexual organs—united—producing a result that is sexless; this must, of course, be the soul, hence it is synonymous with the Roman letter Lux—light. It is the perfect blending of the male and female principles that produces the neuter gender. That the Crux Ansata is a relic of that age when the Phallic religion was prevalent is further proven by the ancient Roman symbols as shown in the cut representing the two goddesses—truth and justice—each holding in her hand the emblem of perfection.

They are worshiping at the altar of the *male* principle, as it is through the *male* principle that the fire of the soul first separates from its unity with God.

It is through man or the male principle that *involution* takes place; through woman, or female, does *evolution* occur.

The labors of a priest tend toward the *evolution* of the race; and how perfectly does he symbolize his work when wearing some of the robes of his office, his head inserted in the oval of the Crux Ansata and the cross hanging down his back.

To the reader of symbols he is the living, active, soul principle; personifying the language of the double symbol he carries.

The symbolism of the Lion's Grip is astronomical, biological and psychological, its main beauty being in the latter sense.

By reference to Chart No. 1 it will be seen that when the earth is in the sign Scorpio, the sun appears to be in the sign Taurus (the Bull). Scorpio is the sign of the sexual organs; it is through them that all conception takes place.

Nine months from conception the earth has moved round through the signs of the Zodiac to Leo and that which was conceived is now brought forth (born) and a *dead thing* (matter) *is raised on the five points of contact.* The soul being a master builder does the work.

The hand is used as a symbol to give the grip as the four fingers represent the four elements: Fire, Earth, Air and Water, while the thumb, the *fifth point,* (the soul) fraternizes with all the fingers, but they, like the elements, do not unite with each other.

The Lion is not only King of Beasts—he is chief of the cat tribe, all of whom see best in the dark.

The soul in its human embodiments is encased in matter (darkness).

The future is unknown. It is metaphorically blindfolded and

therefore seeks the light. Hence the Lion is a symbol of the soul.

In the Egyptian illustration the female figure represents *evolution* commanding *involution* as a principle to rise.

The vacant crown shows that something is still needed to complete the work in hand, a ruling power. The principle of *evolution* symbolized by the female figure, realizes her inability to do the work alone, so with her arm at right angles, describing 90 degrees of a circle, she commands the principle of *involution* personified by her brother to recognize his own soul. He is buried in the world of matter or animal passions, symbolized by the lion (chief of the animal world).

I am loth to leave this subject without shedding some light upon a question which the whole world has asked in vain and to which Masonry itself has so far failed to give satisfactory answer, "Why is woman debarred from membership in the Masonic order?"

If, as brother Brown suggests, the emblem should be adopted by the fraternity it would disrupt the entire teachings of modern Masonry, and would give the woman a moral right to ask for admission, in order that she might assist in carrying out the work sought to be done, as symbolized by the engraving, viz.: Evolution.

Previous to the York Convention, A. D. 926, at which time a Masonic constitution was adopted, the number of degrees was limited to three, and the nature of the work done in the lodges was purely metaphysical, women being as necessary to its accomplishment as men. Then, as to-day, the best metaphysicians, clairvoyants and psychics were women.

I quote from "Encyclopedia of Free Masonry," by Albert G. Mackey, one of the best modern authorities: "The law which excludes women from initiation into Masonry is not contained in the precise words in any of the old constitutions, although it is continually implied, as when it is said in the Landsdowne MS. (year 1560) that the apprentice must be 'of limbs whole as a man ought to be,' and that he must 'be no bond man.'

"All the regulations also refer to men only, and in the charges, compiled by Anderson and published in 1723, the word woman is for the first time introduced and the law is made explicit, as thus it is said that the persons admitted members of a lodge must be good and true *men,* no bond men, no women," etc.

Of course to be in possession of the limbs and *parts* of a man would mean that the candidate be a *cross bearer,* i. e., must have the male sexual organs in full vigor. He must be competent to create, because as a builder of a temple dedicated to God's service he becomes a co-worker with God, the creator of the universe.

But as a symbol the cross represents death: the life of God flows through the male first, which dies in giving up that life to the female who in turn conceives the life and brings it forth.

So long as these two, man and woman, work separately the result of their labors (sexually) is the birth of animals.

In the chapter on digits the Law, symbolized by the figure 6, is the same law that is shown by the Crux Ansata. It means that the recognition by man of his spiritual nature and the recognition by woman of her spiritual self, and then the conscious union of these four in one, produce a result of absolute immunity from the attractions of matter.

Putting words into the mouth of the high priestess in the figure shown she would say:

"Come my brother, see; I have overcome the lusts of the flesh, have subdued the three elements of fire, earth and water. I have travelled over 90 degrees of the circle of infinity. I am life, and can stand erect, but my life is not perfect. I need your crowning power. Recognize me and we shall have life eternal."

Thus does every man's spiritual bride speak to him and beg for recognition and evolution, thus does the spiritual groom of every woman ask to be embraced, received and nurtured, for he is the spirit of God involuting, and has a right to tempt her. In the language of the symbol shown woman could not bear a cross. It would be impossible for her to take the three great degrees of Royal-arch Masonry. She can take two, but she must fail at the third. The first degree, Entered Apprentice, means the point of conception when the soul, a ray of light, enters the temple between the two pillars, father and mother. Nine months later, at birth, it is "raised" to Fellowcraft on the five points of fellowship, and becomes a worker in the Grand Lodge. At the age of twelve years or thereabout, under the ripening influences of the planet Jupiter, the candidate arrives at puberty or is passed to the degree of "master" of life.

It is a stupendous responsibility to be entrusted with the secret creative name of God; it should never be spoken (expressed) except in the presence of two witnesses, spirit and matter.

CHAPTER XXIV.

THE ALL-SEEING EYE.

The Human Soul Born into Matter with the Five Senses Fully Developed for It—These Are Its Working Tools—The Trestle Board of the Soul—The Soul Like Hiram Abif, a Skilled Workman Among Metals—No Sound Except Metallic Sound—Psychometry a Masonic Art—The Origin of Handshaking—Grips, Signs and Passwords May Be Counterfeited, but the Law of the Soul Is Unerring—The Intelligence of the Atom—The Importance of the Atom—Atoms Bear the Imprint and Name of the Form in Which They Are Incorporated—We Are Unconscious of Health, but Awaken to Hunger, Thirst, Disease and Pain—It Was the Sinners Who Were Nearest Approached by Christ—Each Human Being an Atom in the Divine Anatomy—Humanity as a Whole Forms the Skin or Cuticle of the World—The World Itself but an Atom in the Universe of Worlds—Each Individual a Center and the Human Family Its Circumference—How Masonry Intentionally Misleads Its Members—The Truth

Is Not for Those Who Would Misuse It—Truth a Deadly
Thing—Man in Constant and Conscious Communion with
God.

As a symbol the eye may be said to be another way of making
a picture of God.

The worm has no eyes, yet it senses danger through the pores
of its skin. Deep marine life are not always provided with organs
of sight, yet they build, destroy, rear their young, and pass from the
world of existence in surroundings of midnight darkness. *They see
through other organs.* Many specimens of animal and insect life
are bereft of all organs of sensation except, perhaps, two—and many
times only one—that of taste—and by the power of taste alone do they
see all that is necessary for their existence.

Visit any institute for the blind and see how wonderfully the
power of *seeing through the fingers* is being developed by those
bereft of eye sight. Observe how those who are deaf and dumb *hear*
and *speak* through their eyes and fingers.

But we must go deeper into the ways of nature if we would understand the occult laws pictured by this grand symbol.

Man is born into this great universal lodge room with his five
senses fully developed for him. These are his working tools; with
them he daily takes his bearings and determines just where he is.

These are the instruments with which he measures, plans and
determines the work for the day—his trestle board. For whatever the
body (temple) requires must be sensed through some of the physical
organs, and then by the exercise of these same organs the needs of
the body (temple) are secured.

By the cultivation of these faculties danger is apprehended and defeated; joy is contemplated and achieved.

Within the physical body are all the elements of which the earth is composed in a permutated state.

As gold, silver, iron, copper, and many other metals and minerals compose the earth, so these same substances are found in chemicalization in the human body. Were this not true there would be no sensation at all, *for there can be no sound except metallic sound;* in other words, *metals are the basis of all vibration.*

Every soul, therefore, must be a *skilled and cunning workman in metals* before he can be acceptable unto the Lord.

First Kings, vii:13, reads as follows: "And King Solomon sent and fetched Hiram out of Tyre. He was a widow's son of the tribe of Naphtali, and his father was a man of Tyre, a worker in brass; and he was filled with wisdom, and understanding, and *cunning to work all works in brass.* And he came to King Solomon, and wrought all his work."

Second Chronicles, ii:13-14: [Huram of Tyre writes to King Solomon:] "And now I have sent a cunning man endued with understanding, of Huram my father's, the son of a woman of the daughters of Dan, and his father was a man of Tyre, skillful to work in gold, and in silver, in brass, in iron, in stone, and in timber, in purple, in blue, and in fine linen, and in crimson; also to grave any manner of graving, and to find out every device which shall be put to him, with thy cunning men, and with the cunning men of my Lord David thy father."

Huram Abif, as a type or symbol of the Soul, was not only a skilled workman in metals, but he was master of colors as well.

The source of all color is planetary. That is to say each planet has a vibration of its own, or color. There are seven planets in this solar system besides the sun, moon, and earth. They each rush through space at tremendous velocity, producing their own individual note or color. These in turn are taken up by the sun and blended together as one color or note, and we, by the prism and our musical instruments, divide this one color into primary parts: which are seven, and the one great note is divided into seven primary ones. Thus there can be but seven colors and seven notes.

Of course these seven are divided indefinitely because the stars of heaven are infinite.

This skilled and cunning workman was also an engraver on wood and stone; that is to say .he had complete control of those elements.

What are the bones of our bodies but stony substances?

He was a master workman among fine linens. Linen being a vegetable fiber this is a symbolic way of saying, man must select his food from the vegetable kingdom and not poison himself. He must know intuitively what is good for him and what is not.

The All-Seeing Eye is a symbol of psychometry or soul measurement. We develop this power in contact with nature, but more especially in contact with our fellow human than among the trees and flowers. However, there are many natures so sensitive that they can, even blindfolded, describe a tree by holding a chip from it in the hand, or describe a mine by holding a piece of quartz from its mother lode, read a sealed letter, or describe accurately diseases of an absent person by holding in the hand some article touched by the absent one.

The habit of hand shaking had its origin among a fraternity who understood the law of psychometry, and who were forbidden to meet publicly and teach their art. As a protection against being deceived they extended the hand as a challenge to have their thoughts and intentions searched by the light of the soul, in turn demanding to search the other soul.

Passwords, grips and signs may be counterfeited, but the light of the soul is always true and unerring.

Many business men accept and reject propositions according to their *impressions*.

This faculty of soul measurement, when developed in certain directions, amounts to inspiration.

Many a public speaker owes his fame and prosperity to the fact that at some time (the crucial time) he psychometrized or soul-measured his audience. He sensed what they wanted and then launched his own soul forth into the universal soul, and gave back to his listeners that which they had sent out. He gave them what they wanted.

A young man away from home on a hunting trip, wrote at the end of the first day's sport that he had killed seven wild geese. The letter, unopened, was handed to a psychic woman who happened to be visiting at the home at the time. She held the letter in her hand, closed her eyes, and gave a perfect description of the young man dressed in his hunting costume. She described the tent and surroundings of a hunter's camp. She then said she saw the air full of large birds—she could not tell whether they were eagles, hawks, or crows, but anyhow she saw the young man shooting at them and she could see one—two—three fall.

On the young man's return he was told of the psychometric

reading of his letter, upon which he confessed that he had lied to the amount of four geese. Instead of killing seven he had killed only three.

We may speak lies with our lips, we may write lies with ink and paper, we may even live lies to the world, but the soul of man, being of God, speaks the truth wherever it writes its name.

The atoms of matter in the paper and ink received the true thoughts of the young man.

The furniture of a house becomes magnetized or charged with the thoughts and sentiments, health and diseases of its occupants.

Food is blessed or cursed according to the soul conditions of those who prepare it. Whole families (otherwise happy) are sometimes thrown into quarrelsome and diseased conditions by reason of an unhappy, sickly cook in the kitchen.

Thus it will be seen that *blessings* like prayers, must come from the *heart* to be effective.

Foods receive the thought vibrations of those who prepare them; when food is taken into the system the partakers thereof need not be surprised if they become inspired with the hopes, desires and prayers, or the fears, worries and ailments of those who prepared it.

How much more wholesome is that food prepared by mother's dear hands than similar food prepared by the chef of a cafe or hotel? Mother holds the image of each member of the family in loving thought during the entire process. She fills every morsel of food with that deep care and solicitude that only a mother can feel.

On the other hand, hotel food is prepared by machinery mostly, and no thought of love or kindness is worked into it.

Tin cans, wooden boxes and paper packages form no barrier to thought, and if food stuffs do record thought vibrations what kind of influences are carried home from the corner store which is half saloon and half grocery? Think of the vile thoughts and language emanating from the habitues of such a place. Can one expect a healthy, happy, prosperous people who eat the butter, cheese, oil, and milk, loaded with the thought vibrations of such conditions, to continue happy, healthy and prosperous?

The lesson taught by the All-Seeing Eye is that every atom of matter has intelligence. Not human, of course, but atomic intelligence, sufficient for its expression. Therefore the eye becomes the symbol of soul or sensation. From the highest to the lowest wherever sensation is, there God, symbolized by the All-Seeing Eye, may be found.

CHAPTER XXV.

The Reader Is Invited to Test the Truthfulness of the Statements Made in the Preceding Pages by a Joint Exercise of the Will and Breath—A Realization of Life.

By means of symbols the author has striven to prove the existence of a creative principle. In chapter III the positive statement is made that "soul is sexless and therefore creative." It is not within the scope of this volume to make a full expose of the workings of the soul through the generative organs. Public sentiment forbids the telling of the whole truth upon this sacred and intensely interesting subject. There is, however, a practical, every day use that this creative power can be put to. A little practice of a few very simple exercises will prove to any one that God the source of life is not afar off but most fearfully near, and that the fountain of life is not to be sought after but rather *realized*.

There is no place in the whole universe where there is any *more* life than where we are now this very moment. Ages of time will not bring us any nearer the fountain of life than we are at present.

It can only bring us into a more perfect realization of our soul or will power, and this realization must necessarily come through experience.

When the strange man in Idaho said to the author that "intelligent communion between planets was possible," the author rather questioned the truthfulness of the statement. Subsequent experiences of a personal nature have, however, satisfied him that it is a truth.

If the reader wishes to test his own creative power let him first get control over the physical body. Not only the *voluntary* muscles, such as the arms, feet and legs, but the *involuntary* muscles as well, such as the heart, liver, stomach and bowels. Of course there are but few ready to believe that the heart and stomach can be brought into subjugation to the will, but let them follow the simple exercises here given and the discovery will soon be made that man is a creator and that every part of his body is responsibe to soul power. In chapter XX it was shown how every breath is numbered and gendered. It was shown that each incoming breath was masculine and that each outgoing breath was feminine. That our life comes in on the incoming breath and goes out on the outgoing breath.

It was shown that all impurities are expunged on the suspended or outgoing breath. Of course the reader will agree that, so long as there is breath in the body there is life, and if that life can be directed or sent to any or all parts of the body it will of a certainty restore the diseased parts to health. We boldly make the statement that *it is possible to breathe through any and all parts of the body,* and as breath is life it follows as a corollary that if one's life can be intelligently directed to any particular part or portion of the body, then man is of a certainty a creator and has power over death, not absolute power but relative.

In the application of the breath as a healing agent, nature must be consulted and worked with and not against therefore let us begin at the foundation. We have seen that it was the expansion of the *diaphram* that caused the first breath, therefore it is necessary that we learn to breathe from the solar plexus rather than the chest.

This is a simple process and easy of accomplishment. Simply *will* the muscles of the diaphram to expand and at the same time *in-*

hale through the nostrils keeping the mouth closed, taking care that there be no expansion of the chest. When, by practice, this can be accomplished the rest is easy. In order to make sure that you are breathing from the solar plexus it is well to place one hand over the region of the navel and the other over the chest, and if the hand on the chest can detect any heaving or expanding you may know that you are not breathing from the solar plexus.

During the early stages of this practice it is best to lie perfectly flat on the back, and after one has become proficient, then it is easy to breathe from the solar plexus while walking in the street or at work under any and all conditions, and by continued practice it finally becomes second nature, and one breathes from their soul unconsciously and this develops a soul or psychic power that will be astonishing.

Having learned to breathe next step is to learn how to direct the generated life to any desired portion of the body.

Again we seek nature and learn from her how to lay our foundation. She tells us that our bodies are made of the elements of the earth and that our bodies have come from all the four quarters of the universe; that there is a constant tendency on the part of the atoms of our bodies to go back to their original elements. That the only obstacle that prevents the dissolution of our bodies is our will and our breath—once the *will* and *breath* leave the body its particles seek their own level.

Nature also tells us that our bodies, like the earth, have polarity, that our head and feet are polar opposites as well as our hands, and that these four electric and magnetic polarities meet at the center of the body (navel).

Every atom of matter in our bodies is therefore polarized to one of the four quarters of the universe.

If we would harmonize our bodies to the life forces of the universe we can only do so by the power of the *breath* intelligently directed by the *will*.

Again we seek nature and apply our key—(*For man has within him the key to the process by which he may know all there is to know*) we make the discovery that man has a mineral (bone) foundation, that there are seven main entrances or doorways, viz. feet, knees, hips, neck, shoulders, elbows, hands, and that the life forces flowing through the marrows of the bones is liable to escape through any of these doorways. We also learn that there are seven vital internal involuntary organs, viz. the heart, lungs, liver, stomach, bowels, kidneys and sexual organs. We now have a foundation and can intelligently proceed to rebuild and remake our own temple. Again do we go to nature and ask her to reveal to us the first and primal matter, and she answers—"Will" synonymus with "Faith." She says to us that "will" coupled with breath is the beginning of all manifested life. How to use our will and breath then is our next concern. Knowing that the atoms of our bodies are polarized to the four corners of the universe we begin to harmonize them with the spirit of the universe by an exercise of our will *and breath*.

To do this we simply breathe through the seven doorways of the mineral temple from the four corners of the universe by the following process: First take the solar breath by willing the diaphragm to expand and at the same time inhaling through the nostrils. When the body feels full hold the breath, close the eyes and will the life power out through the toes, and at the same time be standing on the toes. Hold this position for a few seconds then stand on the heels imagining the life forces flowing from you through the heels into the earth. While still standing on the toes turn the heels outward and imagine the life forces to flow to the two points of the compass in the direction they point. Now place the feet flat on the floor and then turn the toes out in the same manner the heels were turned. If the breath is not yet exhausted rock back and forth on the heels and toes until you can no longer hold it, then assume a normal position and at the same time let go your breath or exhale. After a respite of one or two breaths treat the knees in the same manner by keeping all parts of the body perfectly still except the knees. They alone are to be exercised and breathed through.

First place the feet closely together, stand erect, take the solar breath as before directed, then spread the knees apart as far as possible *without moving the feet*, then put the knees as close together as possible. Now bring your will to bear and force your knees backward as far as possible taking care that no other part of the body moves. Now bend them forward by stooping as low as you can without moving the feet, and as you rise to the normal position exhale the long pent up breath. Next the hips are to be treated in the same manner. After taking the solar breath just will or imagine, if you please, that your breath now pent up in the center of the body is escaping through the joints of the bones in the direction you bend them, first to the east or right, then to the left or west, then in front, south, and then behind or to the north. It matters not so far as the points of the compass is concerned. The work is accomplished by the will, for the breath being suspended is like the steam in a boiler, and as the steam escapes through the weakest part, so the breath of life will follow the will wheresoever it may be directed.

After treating the hip joints, then treat the neck by moving the head backward, forward, to the right and left, of course holding the breath during the process, then take the shoulder joints and by moving them forward, backward, up and down, they, too, become polarized to the four points of the compass. Next pay your respects to the elbows and hands and when treating the hands, simply extend the arms straight out before you, touch the ends of the thumbs, then when you have taken the solar breath, keep the thumbs in contact but bend the fingers up, then down, then out, and then in; put a strain upon them and turn the fingers as far as possible in each of the directions, as exertion is necessary to cause the life forces to flow from the reservoir in the center out through the extremities. Having directed the river of life in and out through the seven doorways of the *foundation temple,* the next step is to visit the seven internal vital organs.

The stomach being the most responsive to the will power, it is best to begin with it, so with the taking of the solar breath and when the body feels full, simply will the stomach up and at the same time will it to tip forward a little accompanying the thought with an exertion to have it do as you desire, and you will notice a very perceptible movement, then with the same breath will it backward and down, then to the right and then to the left. After the stomach take the bowels and with the breath suspended, lift them up by the power of the will then move them to right and then to the left, turning them around and around, first in one direction and then in the other holding the thought all the time that the breath of life or soul force is flowing from the central reservoir at the solar plexus out through that particular part or organ upon which the will is centered.

In treating the internal organs it must be borne in mind that *no portion of the body should move, but that part or organ that is under treatment.* Even the heart, liver and kidneys, after repeated efforts, will respond to the action of the will and a perceptible movement will be noticed.

To recapitulate:

After taking in the solar breath, hold it and while suspended, will the organ or part to move up, down, in, out, forward, backward, right and left, all the time imagining that the breath of life is flowing through the part or organ as directed by the will, and indeed just such phenomena is taking place. Of course the physical atmosphere comes in through the nostrils and passes out through the openings of the throat; but the breath of life goes and comes according to the power and desire of the will.

Every farmer boy knows that in order to shoulder a sack of wheat he must *hold his breath*. No Paddy on the railroad would attempt to cast a shovelful of earth 20 feet without first *taking a breath, closing the mouth and holding it closed during the exertion.*

Any great effort of the body is always accompanied by a temporary suspension of breathing. No pugilist would attempt to give the knockout blow with an open mouth and on an *exhaling breath*. There is no strength nor power nor life in the body void of breath, and breath of itself is powerless except it be directed and guided by will. We cannot breathe our bodies from one place to another. We cannot will them to go from point to point. We must accompany the breath and the will by an effort, an exertion.

As a child I had to learn the use of feet and legs, hands and arms, but as a man I simply will these members to do my bidding and then I accompany the will by making the effort.

Feet, hands, arms, and legs are seldom attacked by disease, and the reason is because those members are more thoroughly under the dominion of the will as they are constantly receiving the breath of life, it being worked in and through them by the power of the will in almost constant exertion.

To the internal organs that are most vital to our health and happiness, we pay no attention, though they are almost as responsive to our will as other portions of the body.

By following these simple instructions the reader will soon discover that the creative principle or God is fearfully close, that it is possible for one to even stop the most acute pain almost instantly by simply taking the solar breath and then willing the life in and out through the part afflicted.

One soon learns too, how to *commune with God* and be conscious of his own at-one-ment. He will then know what the Son of God meant when he said,—"Lo I stand at the door and knock and if any man shall open I will come in and sup with him."

And now, as I reluctantly draw these pages to a close, I wish again to say to the reader, and I regret that I am not able to write it upon the heart, mind and soul of every human being:

Man has within him the key to the process by which he may know all there is to know.

Printed in the United States
47535LVS00001B/183

9 781564 594648